GUIDE TO PHLAMOUDHI

GUIDE TO PHLAMOUDHI

Joanna S. Smith

MIRIAM AND IRA D. WALLACH ART GALLERY

Columbia University in the City of New York

2005

This publication is issued in conjunction with the exhibition
Settlement and Sanctuary on Cyprus from the Bronze Age to the Middle Ages:
Views from the Columbia University Excavations at Phlamoudhi
held at the Miriam and Ira D. Wallach Art Gallery
Columbia University in the City of New York
20 January through 19 March 2005.

This exhibition and publication have been made possible in part through
an endowment established by Miriam and Ira D. Wallach.

FRONT COVER:
View of Phlamoudhi-*Melissa,* looking south, with Trench 2 in the foreground and Trench 1 at the right

BACK COVER:
View of Phlamoudhi-*Vounari*, looking north

Library of Congress Control Number 2004117142
ISBN 1-884919-17-0

*This guide is dedicated to all
who have contributed
to the archaeology of
the village of Phlamoudhi
and its environs.*

TABLE OF CONTENTS

ACKNOWLEDGMENTS

The Phlamoudhi Archaeological Project is grateful to the following, without whom our work would not have been possible:

Alexander S. Onassis Public Benefit Foundation
Anastasios G. Leventis Foundation
Columbia University Art Properties
Columbia University Center for Archaeology (CCA)
Columbia University Center for Environmental Research and Conservation (CERC)
Columbia University Center for the Ancient Mediterranean (CAM)
Columbia University Council Grant, Hettleman Fellowship
Columbia University Expedition to Phlamoudhi original project members
Columbia University graduate student project participants
Columbia University undergraduate student project participants
Cyprus American Archaeological Research Institute (CAARI)
Cyprus Museum
Department of Antiquities of Cyprus
Department of Art History and Archaeology at Columbia University
Department of Classics at Columbia University
Dr. M. Aylwin Cotton Foundation
Friends of Phlamoudhi
Hunter College undergraduate student project participants
Institute for Aegean Prehistory (INSTAP)
The Metropolitan Museum of Art, Department of Greek and Roman Art
New York University undergraduate student project participants
The Pierpont Morgan Library, Collection of Seals and Tablets
Project volunteers not formally enrolled in a degree program
Samuel H. Kress Foundation
Shelby White – Leon Levy Program for Archaeological Publications

PREFACE

Phlamoudhi is a small village located on the north coast of Cyprus. Most remarkable among the archaeological discoveries there are the sites of *Melissa* and *Vounari*. They preserve unique views into the expanding world of international sea trade in the Mediterranean Late Bronze Age. When I first read about the excavations in the village of Phlamoudhi, while researching my dissertation in 1992 at the Cyprus American Archaeological Research Institute in Nicosia, little did I expect to contribute to their publication or public display. At that time, I wrote to the director of the Columbia University Expedition to Phlamoudhi, Professor Edith Porada, to inquire about some worked bone objects from the excavations. In reply, she kindly referred me to her student Daphne Achilles, who was working on discoveries from *Melissa*.

In 2000, when I came to Columbia to interview for a position in the Department of Art History and Archaeology, Professor Stephen Murray, then the chair, asked me if I knew that the department housed most of the objects found in the Phlamoudhi excavations. He also wondered whether I knew how their publication might be completed and the objects subsequently returned to the Department of Antiquities of Cyprus. When I arrived at Columbia University to teach in the fall of 2000, not only did I encounter the Phlamoudhi material, but also I then met and began to work with Daphne Achilles. She was a considerable help as I began to plan for the publication and exhibition of the discoveries made by the original team in the early 1970s. The exhibition idea came about during an open house for the Phlamoudhi archaeological lab in February 2001. Professor David Rosand inquired whether the discoveries might form the basis for a show in the Miriam and Ira D. Wallach Art Gallery. With the support of Sarah Elliston Weiner and Jeanette Silverthorne of the gallery, that proposed show became a reality.

This *Guide to Phlamoudhi* is modeled on the standard series of Bank of Cyprus Cultural Foundation guidebooks to archaeological sites on Cyprus. It represents the work of countless individuals who have contributed to the original discovery, the study and analysis, and, ultimately, the publication of sites found by the Columbia University Expedition to Phlamoudhi. The guidebook accompanies the Miriam and Ira D. Wallach Art Gallery exhibition *Settlement and Sanctuary on Cyprus from the Bronze Age to the Middle Ages: Views from the Columbia University Excavations at Phlamoudhi* (20 January through 19 March 2005).

Visitors to the exhibition experience simulated visits to the two main sites of *Melissa* and *Vounari*. Photographs, floor plans, maps, and original objects from the excavations highlight the settlements and sanctuaries found there. There are also comparative pieces from the Cesnola Collection of the Metropolitan Museum of Art (Myres 1914: nos. 98, 213, 738, 818, 1046b; Karageorghis et al. 2004: nos. 11, 131, 158, 323), the Pierpont Morgan Library (Porada 1948a: nos. 1049, 1063, 1069), and Columbia University's own collection. In addition, the visitor learns about the history of archaeological work in the village, including tombs excavated and surveys conducted in the region, and the significance of that work for what is known about Cyprus and its role in the eastern Mediterranean over the last four thousand years of human history.

With the guidebook and exhibition, the visitor comes as close to a full visit to the sites as is possible at the present time. Since 1974, the village of Phlamoudhi has not been accessible for systematic archaeological investigation. Should that situation change, the sites could be cleaned, conserved, and opened to the public. Only then could this guide inform a visitor at the actual places described in the following pages.

What we know about ancient Phlamoudhi survives mainly in the written records of the original Columbia expedition, in copious photographs and drawings by the original team and ours, and the thousands of ceramic, terracotta, metal, and stone artifacts uncovered in the excavations. Most of this material is housed at Columbia University in the Department of Art History and Archaeology at the time that I write this book. The objects, brought to Columbia for study in 1973 with a permit from the Department of Antiquities of Cyprus, will be returned to Cyprus after the exhibition closes. The Cyprus Museum, in Nicosia, is currently home to some of the more unusual artifacts. Still more objects from the excavations were originally stored in the schoolhouse in the village of Phlamoudhi and in the museum in Famagusta, Cyprus. Those pieces are assumed now to be lost, although we are fortunate to have photographs and drawings of most of them.

This volume is intended as a general guide to the discoveries made by the original Columbia University Expedition to Phlamoudhi and to the approaches and interpretations of the current Phlamoudhi Archaeological Project. It focuses on the second-millennium-BC settlements of *Melissa* and *Vounari*, their cultural outlook from the north coast of Cyprus, and their roles in artistic, economic, and strategic interconnections in the Mediterranean world. Both places were reoccupied from the Archaic through the Hellenistic period when they served as sanctuaries, possibly indicating parts of the boundaries of contemporary settlements. Surface finds from the Roman, Byzantine, Medieval, and Modern periods attest to occupation of the area right up to the present village of Phlamoudhi. The full results of the archaeological work in the area will appear in volumes to be published by the American Schools of Oriental Research in their Archaeological Reports Series. At the present time, further information about our work may be found on our Web site: www.learn.columbia.edu/phlamoudhi/.

Joanna S. Smith
Director, Phlamoudhi Archaeological Project
November 2004

Mediterranean Sea

0 _____ 15 mi
0 _____ 15 km

• Nitovikla

• Lapithos

• Phlamoudhi
Akanthou
• Ayios Iakovos

Kyrenia Mountains

• Toumba tou Skourou   • Chytroi(Kythrea)

• Ledra   • Salamis
• Enkomi

• Soloi

• Apliki
Ambelikou   • Politiko   • Idalion
• Tamassos

Troodos Mountains

• Marion

• Kition
Hala Sultan Tekke

• Sanida
• Paphos   • Alassa   • Maroni
• Kouklia   Kourion •   • Kalavasos
Amathus •
Episkopi •

a

b

Fig. 1 Map of the eastern Mediterranean, with a map of Cyprus showing the location of Phlamoudhi and other sites

CHRONOLOGICAL TABLE

Akrotiri Phase		ca. 9800 BC
Aceramic Neolithic		8200–5000 BC
Ceramic Neolithic		5000–3900 BC
Chalcolithic		3900–2500/2300 BC
Early Bronze Age (Early Cypriot [EC])		2500/2300–1950 BC
Middle Bronze Age (Middle Cypriot [MC])	I	1950–1850 BC
	II	1850–1750 BC
	III	1750–1650 BC
Late Bronze Age (Late Cypriot [LC])	IA	1650–1550 BC
	IB	1550–1450 BC
	IIA	1450–1375 BC
	IIB	1375–1300 BC
	IIC	1300–1200 BC
	IIIA	1200–1125 BC
	IIIB	1125–1050 BC
Geometric Period (Cypro-Geometric [CG])	I	1050–950 BC
	II	950–850 BC
	III	850–750 BC
Archaic Period (Cypro-Archaic [CA])	I	750–600 BC
	II	600–475 BC
Classical Period (Cypro-Classical [CC])	I	475–400 BC
	II	400–310 BC
Hellenistic Period		310–100 BC
Early Roman Period		100 BC–AD 300
Late Roman Period		AD 300–750
Byzantine Period		AD 750–1191
Medieval Period		AD 1191–1571
Ottoman Period		AD 1571–1878
British Period		AD 1878–1960
Republic of Cyprus		from AD 1960

LOCATION OF PHLAMOUDHI VILLAGE AND NEARBY ARCHAEOLOGICAL SITES

Phlamoudhi village (35°24′N, 33°51.5′E) lies along the north coast of Cyprus in the foothills of the Kyrenia Mountain range. The road into Phlamoudhi descends from the main road through the mountains at Kantara. The village is also accessible via the coastal road from Kyrenia. Although access to archaeological sites in the north is limited and the archaeological sites in Phlamoudhi are not formally open to the public, the places mentioned in this guide are still visible, even though they are overgrown with weeds and shrubs and there are no signs to identify them. The *Vounari* mound is the most easily found because it is a conical hill. It rises off the east side of the road leading north out of Phlamoudhi village, just under one kilometer from the coast (35°24.45′N, 33°51.15′E). *Melissa* is harder to find, being located west of Phlamoudhi village and technically within the far eastern boundary of the village of Akanthou. It is a low rise just over one kilometer from the coast on the east side of a north-south dirt road (35°24.03′N, 33°49.70′E). That road branches off the coast road west of Phlamoudhi village (35°24.67′N, 33°49.88′E). The *Pallouri* tomb is located under a half a kilometer north and west of the *Melissa* site. The *Spilios tou Tsali* rock-cut tomb is east of Phlamoudhi village, along the south side of the coastal road near *Ayios Ioannis* chapel. Further details about the locations of these and other sites in the Phlamoudhi village area can be found in publications by Hector Catling (1962), Sarantis Symeonoglou (1972), Selma Al-Radi (1983), Jack Goodwin (1984), and Sophocles Hadjisavvas (1991), the last having the most detailed published maps.

Fig. 2 Map of the Phlamoudhi region >

I. INTRODUCTION

Cyprus has been part of the international fabric of the Mediterranean world throughout its history. Its wealth of resources and strategic location in the eastern Mediterranean have made it a desirable acquisition by rulers. It has been claimed by or fully integrated into many empires, including the Assyrian, Persian, Ptolemaic, Roman, Byzantine, Venetian, Ottoman, and British. Part of the island's importance derives from the Troodos Mountains, rich in copper, from which Cyprus takes its name. Artisans created weapons, tools, vessels, and ships out of the metals, stones, clays, and wood of the island. The cultivation of grains, including flax, and the herding of animals, including sheep, provided fibers for linen and woolen textiles. These fabrics were dyed many colors, including royal purple extracted from the murex. Over the long history of Cyprus, grains, olives and olive oil, salt, and sugar cane were among the wealth of products that reached its Mediterranean neighbors and beyond.

Archaeological investigations in the village of Phlamoudhi offer new perspectives on the island and its international connections during the last four thousand years. Located north of the Kyrenia Mountain range, Phlamoudi is separated from the rich copper resources of the island by this formidable geographic barrier. The occupants of the Phlamoudhi area created unique artistic forms and developed a distinct regional identity. Accounting systems and locally made ceramics attest to close relations with Cilicia to the north, places on and near the Orontes River to the east, and in the Levant. Inhabitants also had access to oils, tablewares, stones, and metals from throughout the Mediterranean, from the Levant to the Aegean and points farther west.

Evidence, albeit scant, shows that life in the Phlamoudhi area extends back into the Neolithic period. The best-preserved of the prehistoric settlements, however, date to the second millennium BC, particularly the Late Bronze Age. This period witnessed improvements in seafaring technology and led to the regular involvement of Cyprus in the exchange of artistic ideas and commodities with the Near East, the Aegean, the Levant, and Egypt. The area was reoccupied in the first millennium BC, when settlements of the Bronze Age were rediscovered and

15

marked as if they were part of a legendary past. As in other parts of the Mediterranean, these Bronze Age places were used as sanctuaries, where worshippers left votives for their gods. Tombs, buildings, and scatters of pottery sherds attest to the lives of people in the area of Phlamoudhi village right up to the present day.

The Columbia University Expedition to Phlamoudhi

On 9 March 1970, Dr. Vassos Karageorghis, then Director of Antiquities of Cyprus, signed a license for excavation at Phlamoudhi-*Vounari*. With this permit, the Columbia University Expedition to Phlamoudhi began its archaeological excavations and survey in and around the village of Phlamoudhi. The project was generously supported by the Harold H. Weekes Fund, which was set up by Mrs. C. B. (Happy) Scully, the daughter of Harold Weekes and a close friend of Profes-

Fig. 3 Participants in the Columbia University Expedition to Phlamoudhi, with *Vounari* in the background, 1972

sor Edith Porada, the director of the expedition. Edith Porada appointed Dr. Sarantis Symeonoglou as the field director.

One of Edith Porada's aims was to provide excavation experience for her graduate students (fig. 3). Many of them, in addition to other students and specialists in photography, architecture, faunal analysis, and other fields, joined the project on Cyprus and worked on the discoveries after they were brought to New York: Daphne Achilles, Charles Adelman, James Allen, Selma Al-Radi, Dimitri Anson, Susan Bodenstein, Ian Cohn, Mr. and Mrs. Angel Coronado, Mary Dabney, Anne Donadeo, Sally Dunham, Allan Gilbert, Joseph Giuliano, Judson Harward, Teresa Hersch, Brian Hesse, Webb Keane, Helen Merrillees, Robert S. Merrillees, Richard Moore, Anne Ogilvy, Samuel Paley, Holly Pittman, Corethia Qualls, Donald Sanders, Jeffrey Schwartz, Happy Scully, Rheba Symeonoglou, Javier Teixidor, Paula Wapnish, and Lin Welden.

Fieldwork took place from 1970 to 1973, when excavations were halted and work on their publication began. The team expected to return to complete architectural plans and the study of objects stored in the village schoolhouse in 1974. Sadly, the invasion of that year and the occupation of the area by the Turkish military put an end to fieldwork in Phlamoudhi. The villagers, with whom the team worked closely during their field seasons, abandoned Phlamoudhi and moved to the southern part of the island or left Cyprus entirely. It is possible to study the results of their fieldwork today because the field notebooks, photographs, maps, find cards, and other records survive along with thousands of objects unearthed in the excavations. In 1973, the project was given the rare permission to export the majority of the finds to New York for study and illustration in preparation for their publication. Had it not been for this export, only a tiny portion of the work on the excavations since 1973 would have been possible.

Edith Porada was an eminent scholar of ancient Near Eastern art history and archaeology at Columbia University (Pittman 1995). She became interested in the art and archaeology of Cyprus through her study of cylinder seals. In two landmark publications in 1948, she published the collection of cylinder seals of the Pierpont Morgan Library (1948a) in New York and, in an article for the *American Journal of Archaeology* (1948b), laid the foundation for all future studies of

Cypriot cylinder seals. Seals, usually of stone, are only a few centimeters in size. They were worn as amulets and used as markers of one's authority or responsibility in economic, legal, and political matters. They come in many shapes, some with a flat carved surface and others, called cylinder seals, with a surface that provides for a continuous horizontal field of decoration. The finely carved intaglio design on cylinder seals was impressed, usually by rolling, onto a clay or other soft surface. In Cypriot seals, Edith Porada recognized antecedents in Syrian seals from the Middle Bronze Age combined with sensibilities derived from Minoan and Mycenaean figural art.

About the Phlamoudhi excavations, Porada wrote that "our aim was to excavate a settlement of the Middle Bronze Age in the hope of finding relations between Western Asiatic and Aegean sites, for which Cyprus might have been an intermediary" (Al-Radi 1983: unnumbered, preface). In 1973, Sally Dunham unearthed a single cylinder seal in a mixed deposit dating to the Late Cypriot II period (fig. 4). Its design is emblematic of Porada's ideas about interconnections in Cypriot art of the artistic styles of the Near East and the Aegean. Appropriately enough, the centerpiece of the design is a lion, the mascot of Columbia University.

In her preliminary publication of the seal, Porada pointed out that "the Near Eastern manner was meant to maintain a lasting stage; the Aegean, to show life in motion" (1986: 294). As the impression shows, a lion is firmly anchored in the design, with a winged sun disk at the top. None of the other creatures or symbols appears to be fixed within the scene. The lion reaches out to claw a bull; the bull, with its horns spearing the foreleg of the lion, strides beyond the groundline of the seal; the griffon rears up its head in response to the contest below; and the goat gallops away as fast as its legs will take it. All the activity is set within a celestially symbolic marine environment. Not only does the design embody Porada's identification of an international style in Cypriot seals, but it mirrors Phlamoudhi's position in the second millennium BC: Phlamoudhi was a constant as well as an active participant in the Mediterranean world at a time when celestial navigation in the open sea was becoming increasingly important.

The Columbia University Expedition achieved, even exceeded, Edith Porada's initial research and educational goals. What was discovered during four

Fig. 4
Hematite cylinder
seal from *Melissa*
and a modern
impression

years of fieldwork included two major sites that were excavated, a large settlement at *Melissa* and a hilltop building at *Vounari*, as well as tombs and surface scatters of ceramic, terracotta, stone, and glass objects. To be sure, some of the remains in the vicinity of Phlamoudhi village had been known prior to the arrival of the Columbia team. For example, Hector Catling recorded and visited the *Vounari* hill and the *Sapilou* site in 1952, which together with a site called *Gouppes* appeared in his seminal article about Bronze Age Cypriot settlement patterns (1962: 168).

In 1970, the Columbia team investigated the *Vounari* hill, as stipulated in the original license to excavate. *Vounari*, meaning "conical hill," is a prominent place visible to anyone walking, riding, or driving between the village of Phlamoudhi and the seacoast. As with other archaeological sites on Cyprus, Phlamoudhi-*Vounari* is named after the village and the locality or field in which the site is to be found.

Initially, the team thought that *Vounari* was a Middle Bronze Age fortification, as proposed by Catling and others. The Columbia excavations, however, showed that it also had a significant Late Bronze Age component as well as Archaic and Hellenistic remains. The team determined that they had found a sanctuary rather than a fortification. Therefore, in 1971, they set out to restudy the context of *Vounari* by conducting a survey of the Phlamoudhi region in order to "learn about the archaeological history of this isolated area" (Symeonoglou 1972: 187).

The survey, led by Sarantis Symeonoglou, recorded a total of thirty-six sites, including the *Vounari* hill. Others were *Melissa*, the settlement site that the team began to excavate that same year, and *Sapilou,* which had previously been located by Catling. Only the most cursory of excavations at *Sapilou* took place before the larger-scale excavations at *Melissa* began. *Melissa*, a name that may refer to honey supplies and possibly beekeeping activity, turned out to be a place with two meters of occupational debris. Most of it comes from more than 550 years of activity in and around a large administrative building with associated ceramic, metal, and other workshops of the Bronze Age. Remains just under and on the surface come from the Archaic period and later.

The earliest of the places located in the survey was *Lakkos*, on the coast north of the *Melissa* settlement. Evidence for its use in the Neolithic period could not be substantiated by the team, although Porphyrios Dikaios had previously reported finding Neolithic stone tools (Ibid.: 190). Nicholas Stanley Price also identified *Lakkos* among other prehistoric sites in the region (1979: 119, F2). A tomb of the late Archaic and early Classical period was found at the site of *Pallouri* (Symeonoglou 1972: 195) and excavated by Edith Porada and Happy Scully (fig. 5). A rock-cut tomb of the Hellenistic period was located at *Spilios tou Tsali* (fig. 6) (Ibid.), which had previously been identified by D. G. Hogarth, who published it with a plan (1889: 99–101).

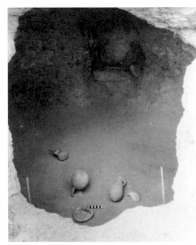

Fig. 5 Phlamoudhi-*Pallouri,* as viewed through a hole in the roof

Among the many other intriguing places found are *Angaremenos,* which may have had a pottery workshop in use as early as the Roman period (Symeonoglou 1972: 193), and natural salt pools at *Limnionoudhi,* which may have been exploited in the Byzantine period (Ibid.: 194). Standing remains of another Hellenistic tomb at *Tsonia* and a church near the Bronze Age *Melissa* site (Ibid.: 193–94) are also particularly noteworthy. Symeonoglou writes that "the present inhabitants of Phlamoudhi still remember that their ancestors moved . . . from *Melissa*. Like other villages in the area, Phlamoudhi was built behind a large hill (called *Vigla,* which means lookout hill), to hide it from pirates. *Melissa* was probably abandoned after the island became part of the Ottoman Empire in 1571" (Ibid.: 193).

Excavations at *Vounari* and *Melissa* continued in 1972 and 1973. The work was conducted in a stratigraphic manner, with the sites divided into different trenches, or zones of excavation. For each trench, as horizontal layers of earth were removed, a section of the earth cut through was kept as a reference on all sides, forming dividers or baulks of earth between the trenches. Deposits or loci of earth, ash, stone, and other material were removed, with attention to the sequence of their deposition in the ground. Because careful records were kept and the pottery and other objects were labeled according to the loci in which they were found, it is possible to reconstruct the building phases, periods of destruction and abandonment, and the activities of the people who occupied ancient *Vounari* and *Melissa.*

The team recorded all the ceramic, stone, glass, and other man-made objects and kept samples or selections of the most identifiable or diagnostic pieces, such as painted sherds and the handles, rims, and bases of vessels. In addition, the Columbia project collected animal bones and ancient plant materials. Allan Gilbert, who worked at the *Melissa* site, introduced water sieving or flotation, which allowed for the retrieval of tiny remains of fish and even figs. After the excavations, he and others embarked on some preliminary scientific analyses, including neutron-activation analysis and thin-section studies of the ceramics, to determine their chemical and mineralogical composition, possible points of origin, and similarity to other contemporary ceramics. These studies are still under way.

Fig. 6 Hellenistic rock-cut tomb at Phlamoudhi-*Spilios tou Tsali*

Following each season of excavation, the more unusual objects, including the cylinder seal, some of the bronze finds, the limestone and terracotta figurines and statuettes, and a selection of large stone and terracotta tools and vessels were deposited in the Cyprus Museum. One large stone vessel found in 1971 went to the Famagusta Museum. All other finds were brought back to Columbia University with the exception of some ceramic vessels, many of the stone tools, most of the glass fragments, and a few fragments of ivory, metal, and terracotta that were stored in the schoolhouse in the village of Phlamoudhi. Once the finds and records were in New York, their study commenced in laboratory space at the university. The lab has moved several times between 1973 and 2004. Today, most of the items brought to Columbia are still together as a collection, with the exception of some of the animal bones that remain to be located.

Some of the excavation results were published by the original Columbia team. An article on the animal bone by Brian Hesse, Anne Ogilvy, and Paula Wapnish appeared in the *Report of the Department of Antiquities, Cyprus* (1975). Most notably, Selma Al-Radi published the essentials of the architecture and stratigraphy for the site of *Vounari* in 1983. That volume also contained a report on faunal remains (Hesse et al. 1983). Edith Porada published the cylinder seal in 1986. Some of the scientific studies based on the sherd material appeared in articles by Sarah Vaughan (1991a, b) and in a volume about the provenience of Bronze Age objects (Knapp and Cherry 1994).

In 1991, a separate project that also pertains to Phlamoudhi appeared. Sophocles Hadjisavvas published the results of surveys by the Bureau for the Establishment of the Inventory of the Cultural Property of Cyprus. Although this inventory, begun in 1973, had to be left incomplete because of the events of 1974, the volume nevertheless contains clear maps and important information for the area of Phlamoudhi (1991: 14–21) and surrounding villages, including Akanthou (Ibid.: 1–13), the village in which the *Melissa*, *Lakkos*, *Pallouri*, and *Angaremenos* sites technically are located.

The Phlamoudhi Archaeological Project

In 2000, I worked with students at Columbia University to launch a new campaign to complete the publication of the Columbia University Expedition to Phlamoudhi. To distinguish between the original project's contributions and our analyses and interpretations, this project was called the Phlamoudhi Archaeological Project. First, we set up a new lab space with the help of Daphne Achilles. She, Allan Gilbert, and Robert Merrillees proved to be invaluable sources of information about the original project. Sally Dunham, Samuel Paley, Holly Pittman, and other original team members have also contributed to our understanding.

Although I did not direct the original excavation of the archaeological sites, the current project has been, nonetheless, an excavation as well as a survey. Becoming familiar with the notes and discoveries made by other people necessitated rediscovering objects housed in different parts of the Columbia University campus and in the Cyprus Museum. By reading and analyzing the notes, I have tried to understand as much as possible of the thought process of the original Columbia University Expedition to Phlamoudhi. Using their detailed records, I have been able to formulate my own hypotheses about the artistic, economic, regional, and international significance of the findings. And, in the case of *Melissa*, I reconstructed more than ten periods of occupation rather than the two proposed by the original team.

Being prevented from returning to the sites to record or clean them has been both a blessing and curse. It would have been preferable, for example, to go to *Melissa* and complete the architectural plan of the excavations prior to publication. Had we had the opportunity to clean the sites, however, it would have been irresistible to apply for permits to test, through excavation, some of the more enigmatic parts of the excavated areas. By not having access, it has been easier to focus on completing the publication. We have thus been able to address a long-standing interest of the Department of Antiquities of Cyprus, as well as other professional organizations such as the Archaeological Institute of America and the American Schools of Oriental Research: completing the publication of an old excavation and making the results known to the public.

We were pleased to receive the permission and support of the Department of Antiquities of Cyprus. Just after the new project got under way, I received a letter dated 9 February 2001 from Dr. Despo Pilides, written on behalf of the director of the Department of Antiquities. She called the publication of the material at Columbia University from the excavations at Phlamoudhi-*Melissa* "excellent news." "As you know we have been focusing our efforts for some time now on arousing interest amongst excavators/archaeologists to publish the material from old, unpublished excavations. Consequently, your proposal to publish the material from Phlamoudhi is particularly welcome."

Several undergraduate and graduate students as well as nonstudent volunteers have contributed significantly to the Phlamoudhi Archaeological Project. Those who have served as long-term lab assistants and/or full summer season team members are Carolyn Bancroft, Ellen Blount, Anna Browne-Ribeiro, Roberta Casagrande-Kim, Nancy Dammann-Davis, Todd Davis, Mara Horowitz, Kyle Killian, Sandrine Larrivé-Bass, Martina Mims, Lauren Rogers, Elizabeth Sanseau, Polly Tessler, Amy Tjiong, Courtney Tomaselli, and Lee Ullmann. Dr. David Reese has conducted independent research on the bone and shell collections. Reconstructions of some of the most complete vessels that appear in the exhibition were done in part by Daphne Achilles prior to 2000, but more recent conservation efforts were contributed by Catherine Sease of the Peabody Museum at Yale University and Carola Garcia Manzano, an independent conservator.

Our first concern was to examine the tens of thousands of ceramic fragments from the *Melissa* excavations. Kyle Killian agreed to study and publish the Hellenistic, Roman, Byzantine, Medieval, and Modern ceramics, most of which came from surface deposits. For research on the Middle to Late Bronze Age and the Archaic to Classical ceramics, the lab was open one day a week during the semesters and for one entire month in the summer of 2002 (fig. 7). I used the collection as an on-campus archaeological experience for students to learn how to work with archaeological ceramics. It was during that period that I recognized evidence for Bronze Age ceramic manufacture at *Melissa*.

The work at Columbia continued through 2004 with ceramic and small find illustration, with original records to reconstruct the stratigraphy, and with the preparation for this exhibition. In 2003, I took a small group to the Cyprus Museum to study stone and bronze tools, precious stone beads, limestone and terracotta sculptures, some ceramics, and ancient plant remains from the *Melissa*, *Vounari*, *Pallouri*, and *Marikou* sites. We also had our first opportunity to visit the village of Phlamoudhi. Dr. Robert Merrillees, who had been part of the original expedition, accompanied us to Phlamoudhi. We found the schoolhouse and the *Vounari* site. At the time of our visit, free travel across the United Nations green line was only just beginning. Official permission for our trip from the Department of Antiquities was not possible, but we were pleased to learn that any photographs that we took during our visit could be used to document the sites and could appear in our publications. It was not until 2004 that two members of my team, Lee Ullmann and Mara Horowitz, relocated *Melissa*. It was good to know that the sites

Fig. 7 Members of the Phlamoudhi Archaeological Project, at the Metropolitan Museum of Art, 2002

are still there, should the opportunity appear to return to Phlamoudhi and complete the recording begun in the early 1970s.

Also in 2003, Mara Horowitz embarked on a study of the ceramics from *Vounari* and a restudy of that site's architecture and stratigraphy for her Ph.D. dissertation. In the course of her work, she has challenged the identification of *Vounari* solely as a cult place in the Bronze Age. We think now that its monumental building served as a storage center and transfer point along a northern trade route of which *Melissa* was also a part.

II. CYPRUS IN THE SECOND MILLENNIUM BC

The second millennium BC in the Mediterranean was a period of vibrant artistic innovation, magnificent royal palaces, entrepreneurial trading ventures, and an increasing focus on the Mediterranean Sea as a place to travel in rather than around. As shipping technology improved, with larger and sturdier boats, it was possible for ports of trade on the island of Cyprus to become regular destinations rather than occasional stopping points. It also meant that there was an increased need to protect coastal interests against pirate raids, particularly along parts of the island that were closest to important trading centers in southeastern Anatolia and northern Syria.

During this time, Cyprus grew from isolated villages and towns into a place characterized by a series of urban coastal centers (Merrillees 1992; Keswani 1996; Knapp 1997), one of the most important of which was fifteen hectares. No one place appears to have wielded authority over the entire island. Furthermore, urban centers tended to be set back at least a kilometer from the coast. Each center formed part of a network of towns, villages, ports, and temporary workshops near sources of raw materials. These networks followed river routes, normally between the copper-rich Troodos Mountains and the sea. In this way each center potentially had access to metal ores as well as water, agricultural land, trees, clays, and other natural resources important for sustaining daily life and supporting on-island as well as international exchange.

As Cyprus became a regular participant in economic, political, and artistic contacts among Near Eastern, Aegean, Anatolian, and Egyptian powers, its people, buildings, household objects, cults, and written communications began to reflect the island's international orientation. Each center emerged with its own artistic profile, differing in the details of its local architecture, ceramics, personal emblems such as cylinder seals, forms of writing in the island's Cypro-Minoan script, and taste for imported objects. Even with the differences, there was enough similarity that those who traveled among the urban centers would have recognized the places as culturally Cypriot, with identifiable settlements, sanctuaries, and cemeteries, and in some way part of the cosmopolitan world of the Mediterranean.

Toward the end of the Bronze Age, circa 1200 BC, destructions of palaces and peoples across the Mediterranean, by earthquake, invasion, famine, and other disasters, brought an end to part of the Mediterranean sea traffic. The royal face of international exchange now reflected more of the merchantmen who owned and maintained many of the ships. At this time, some small urban centers in Cyprus, with their networks of towns and villages, were abandoned. Interestingly, however, the population of the island did not disperse but moved into significantly expanded cities, places that grew to be approximately one hundred hectares in size.

One of these cities, Kition, which now lies below the modern city of Larnaca, embodies this change (Karageorghis and Demas 1985). Excavations there by the Department of Antiquities under the direction of Vassos Karageorghis demonstrated that Kition, instead of being set back from the coast, lay directly at the harbor. While it must still have relied on a network of towns and villages, including the approximately twenty-five-hectare center of Hala Sultan Tekke to the south (Åström 1989), Kition became one of the preeminent centers of trade in the Mediterranean, a role it continued to play in subsequent centuries when it was a Phoenician center of power. Depictions of ships on temples at its port, as well as large textile, dye, and metal workshops, begin to create a picture of Kition's involvement in shipping in the years following the total or near ruin of the powerful kings of the Hittites, Syria, Egypt, and the Mycenaean world.

What Cyprus or any of these urban centers was called and who was in control of politics in the Late Bronze Age is a puzzle. The texts from the island, written in a script called Cypro-Minoan, remain undeciphered (Palaima 1989). They are a mix of signs based on the undeciphered writing of Minoan Crete, Linear A, and handwriting styles typical of Near Eastern wedge-shaped, or cuneiform, writing, as well as the calligraphic style of Aegean scribes (Smith 2003). While we recognize that the script includes numbers, logograms or word signs, and signs that represent syllables, we have yet to read the documents phonetically. No documents from Cyprus written in Near Eastern or Aegean languages offer any further evidence.

Beginning in the eighteenth century BC with texts from places such as King Zimri-Lim's palace at Mari, however, we read of a place called Alashiya. Alashiya continues to appear in Mesopotamian, Hittite, Syrian, Egyptian, and even Mycenaean documents (Knapp 1996). That place lay somewhere along the

Mediterranean coast and had access to vast quantities of copper from Mount Taggata. Because of the rich copper resources of Cyprus, most scholars make an equation between Alashiya and some part of the island. It is unclear, however, whether Alashiya was on an island or the mainland. Wherever it was, Alashiya appears to have survived the destructions of palace centers at the end of the Bronze Age, for it features in the eleventh-century *Tale of Wenamun*.

Scholars have proposed several candidates for the location of Alashiya on Cyprus. The fifteen-hectare urban center of Enkomi-*Ayios Iakovos* near the east coast of the island has been favored because of its position directly across the Mediterranean from the city of Ugarit, a major coastal seaport. Documents at Ugarit suggest that Alashiya could be seen from there. Furthermore, the French archaeologist Claude F. A. Schaeffer, who excavated both at Enkomi and at Ugarit, made the Alashiya link even stronger; he used the name Alashiya in the titles of his Enkomi publications: *Enkomi-Alasia I* (1952) and *Alasia* (1971).

Kouklia, in the west near the city of Paphos, was originally thought to have been a candidate, based on the sourcing of clay from the documents that were sent from Alashiya to the Eighteenth-Dynasty pharaoh Akhenaten in the fourteenth century BC (Artzy et al. 1976). New studies of the clay sources for those documents, however, support two more recently excavated sites as candidates for Alashiya, Kalavasos-*Ayios Dhimitrios* near the south coast and Alassa (Goren et al. 2003) in the foothills of the Troodos Mountains north of the site of Episkopi-*Bamboula*. Of all of these places, the only one that was settled densely for the full period of time that Bronze Age Alashiya appears to have existed is Enkomi. Possibly, however, Alashiya refers not to one single place but to different places at different points in time during the Bronze Age.

Of these and other urban centers that formed parts of Cyprus in the Late Bronze Age, we tend to have views at only one or a few points in time. If one of these sites, or a succession of sites, does turn out to be Alashiya, we have but a fractional view. It is hard to find a site that has evidence for occupation for the entire period that Alashiya is thought to have been a power and for which we have well-recorded and published excavation evidence.

The best-known place on Cyprus from the Late Bronze Age is Enkomi, near the east coast. Hundreds of wealthy tombs, a town plan with a grid of streets, large and small residences, workshops, sanctuaries, and a city wall have all been uncovered. Nearly a quarter of the site has been excavated since the nineteenth century: by a team from the British Museum (Murray et al. 1900), by the Swedish Cyprus Expedition (Gjerstad et al. 1934), by a French team led by Claude F. A. Schaeffer (1952, 1971; Courtois et al. 1986), and by the Department of Antiquities of Cyprus under the Direction of Porphyrios Dikaios (1969, 1971). The work by the British, Swedish, and Cypriot teams has been published, but areas uncovered by the French may remain only partly published. At Enkomi we have a view into approximately seven hundred years of Middle and Late Bronze Age life on Cyprus. Unfortunately, the vast horizontal area uncovered reveals only partially how the town grew and changed over its long history. Our best glimpses come from areas excavated by the Department of Antiquities, where evidence has been found for how a fortified site grew into a larger, more cosmopolitan city.

Kouklia, or Palaepaphos, just east of the modern city of Paphos, was the cult center of the great goddess of Cyprus who was later called Aphrodite (Maier 1975). Palaepaphos was known already at the end of the nineteenth century (Maier and Karageorghis 1984); most of the work there was conducted by Luigi Palma di Cesnola, the Cyprus Exploration Fund, the British Kouklia Mission, the Department of Antiquities under the direction of Vassos Karageorghis, a team led by Franz Georg Maier of the University of Zurich and the German Archaeological Institute, and the Canadian Palaepaphos Survey Project led by David Rupp (Sørensen and Rupp 1983). Surveys and excavations suggest that Kouklia reached the size of Kition. Most notable are the sanctuary of the goddess, some well deposits, and a series of wealthy tombs. Given the size and the prominence of its cult center, Kouklia came to be recognized across the Mediterranean in the years following 1200 BC and was probably a significant urban place even before then.

Kalavasos-*Ayios Dhimitrios* and Alassa are more recently excavated Late Bronze Age sites (Hadjisavvas 2003). Kalavasos-*Ayios Dhimitrios* was discovered in 1979 during construction of a new highway along the south coast of the island. Excavations by Alison South and Ian Todd have brought to light an approximately twelve-hectare urban center with evidence for wealthy tombs, a gridded street pattern, workshops, residences, and a substantial administrative building, called Building X (South 1989; South et al. 1989). Of all the candidates for Alashiya, Kalavasos-*Ayios Dhimitrios* preserves the most detailed evidence for written economic records or administrative affairs, but the inscriptions appear to concern local accounts and are in the context of the vast storage of olive oil rather than metals (Smith 2002b). Part of Building X housed large ceramic storage vessels called pithoi, some reaching two meters in height (Keswani 1989; Pilides 2000). To the west of Building X, Building XI housed a pressing area and a stone collection vat. The collection vat and interiors of a sampling of the pithoi were analyzed using gas chromatography, which showed that they had contained olive oil (South 1992).

Alassa and its two major sites of *Palaeotaverna* and *Pano Mandilaris* became the focus of systematic archaeological investigation by Sophocles Hadjisavvas of the Department of Antiquities of Cyprus in 1983, when the village of Alassa was slated to be inundated with water from a new dam and reservoir (Hadjisavvas 1989, 2003). Today the sites are above the water level and will apparently remain out of danger. At Alassa-*Palaeotaverna,* a large building constructed with carefully hewn, or ashlar, blocks rivals Building X in sheer size. As with Building X, the Alassa structure contained many pithoi. Alassa-*Pano Mandilaris* preserves the larger urban fabric of which *Palaeotaverna* was a part.

Work at Alassa thus provides information about a place that lies north of another large urban center that is also on the Kouris River but nearer to the coast: Episkopi-*Bamboula* (Benson 1972; Weinberg 1983). Episkopi-*Bamboula* was excavated beginning in 1937 by John Franklin Daniel of the University of Pennsylvania. New excavations there are under the direction of Gisela Walberg of the University of Cincinnati. I have observed that Alassa and Episkopi, in addition to their geographic proximity, were also related administratively: the same cylindrical wooden roller, a large form of a cylinder seal, bearing a series of carved griffins, was used to mark storage pithoi from both sites (Benson 1956: fig. 6, no. Sh580; Hadjisavvas 2001: fig. 8, no. 1995/10). With the exception of *Vounari* and *Melissa* at Phlamoudhi, these sites are the only ones that are connected demonstrably in their economic administration by the sphragistic use of the same seal.

These and other Cypriot urban centers, such as Maroni on the south coast

(Cadogan 1989; Manning et al. 2002) and Toumba tou Skourou in the Ovgos River Valley (Vermeule and Wolsky 1990), inform us about the form, function, and administrative associations among large urban population centers in the second millennium BC. Enkomi is our most promising window into the full length of time that people lived there. At Kouklia, we can piece together the past from disparate, mainly funerary, sources. At Kalavasos and Alassa, we have views largely into their final forms rather than how they grew to be densely inhabited areas of economic and, possibly, political importance.

The question remains, however, of the nature of urban expansion on Cyprus during the period represented by the references to Alashiya. Whether or not Alashiya was in fact related to Cyprus, the period from the eighteenth through the eleventh century BC represents one of urban growth and ultimately consolidation that led to a preeminent role for Cyprus in the exchange of objects, commodities, and artistic ideas throughout the Mediterranean. Discoveries to date make clear that there were central administrative buildings, some large centers were connected regionally through a common administration, and urban centers were active in international trade. Thus far, however, we have no lush palaces similar to those in other parts of the Mediterranean that accommodated apartments for royal families who ruled for generations and commanded large households. There is also no sign of a place for the public to have an audience with a ruler. No less wealthy than their neighbors in their material possessions, the Cypriots of the second millennium BC who organized and benefited from the booming economy appear to have been spread throughout Cypriot society. In order to understand the development of the urban form and way of life on Cyprus during the second millennium BC, it is important to consider a well-excavated place through the entire period from the eighteenth century to the end of the Bronze Age.

Further, it is important to question the significance of copper as a defining element for Cypriot Late Bronze Age society. Although commonly assumed, it remains to be shown that the central role of the copper industry was in fact a key feature of urban expansion on the island. Areas of copper mining and smelting, such as Ambelikou-*Aletri* in the Middle Bronze Age (Merrillees 1984) and Politiko-*Phorades* in the Late Bronze Age (Knapp et al. 2001), are few and do not give us a view into the large-scale and permanent islandwide industry that is often a descriptor of second-millennium-BC Cyprus. At urban centers near the coasts, the evidence for copper working consists of the melting of copper and even the recycling of bronze rather than the original smelting of copper ore (Karageorghis and Kassianidou 1999). Nevertheless, Cypriot copper was mined in large enough quantities to make ingots weighing approximately twenty-six kilograms each, which formed significant parts of the cargo on ships, such as the one that sank off the coast of Ulu Burun, Turkey, at the end of the fourteenth century BC (Pulak 2001). Recent research about the Late Bronze Age copper-working site of Apliki-*Karamallos*, excavated by Joan du Plat Taylor in the 1930s (du Plat Taylor 1952; Kling and Muhly nd); survey work by the Sydney Cyprus Survey Project (Given and Knapp 2003) and now the Troodos Archaeological and Environmental Survey Project (Given and Knapp 2001); and archaeometallurgical studies across the island suggest that mining and smithing were just as regional as many other artistic and industrial endeavors of people during the second millennium BC.

Phlamoudhi-Melissa

The Columbia University Expedition to Phlamoudhi unearthed evidence for two sites that preserve views into the growth and development of an urban landscape from the eighteenth through the thirteenth century BC. Phlamoudhi-*Melissa,* together with the neighboring site of Phlamoudhi-*Vounari,* provides unique perspectives on urban development that was not based on the direct exploitation of or control over any part of the copper resources of the Troodos Mountains. These two places were linked economically, culturally, and visually. Each could be seen easily from the other. *Vounari* was the more prominent place in the landscape due to its elevation on a natural hill. It can be seen as one descends from the Kyrenia Mountains, as one approaches from the sea, and as one travels across the foothills and the north shore of Cyprus. By contrast, *Melissa* was hidden from many points of view. Its location may have been selected purposely to put it out of sight, protecting it from land and sea raids and making the safekeeping of food supplies and industries easier.

Melissa is a large habitation site with evidence for occupation in the second millennium BC from the Middle Cypriot III period through the end of the Late Cypriot IIC period (fig. 8). Building and other activity at the site during this period falls into eight stages:

Preconstruction	Middle Cypriot III
Phase 1	Middle Cypriot III (new building)
Phase 2	Late Cypriot IA (building remodeled)
Phase 3	Late Cypriot IB (building remodeled)
Phase 4	Late Cypriot IIA (building remodeled and expanded)
Phase 5	Late Cypriot IIB (building remodeled, expanded, burned)
Phase 6	Late Cypriot IIC [with Phase 7 as a small remodeling] (building remodeled, expanded, burned)

What survives is one corner of a large building that was constructed and expanded at least seven times during the Bronze Age. It is a rectilinear building with stone and mudbrick walls that were roofed with beams cut from pine, olive,

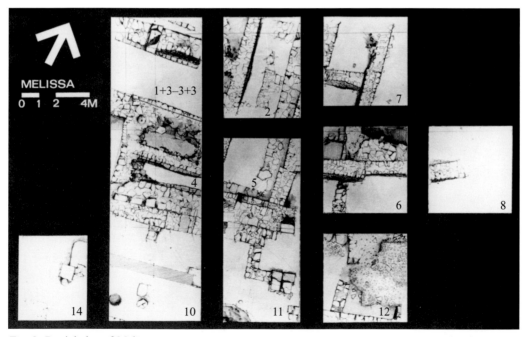

Fig. 8 Partial plan of *Melissa*

33

and other local hardwood trees (Dammann-Davis nd). The later structure used finely hewn, or ashlar, stone masonry in some parts, possibly those that needed greater support or were more visible. A pillar in the southern area of the Phase 6 building once supported a finely carved capital. As the building was built and rebuilt, some floors and walls were covered with lime plaster.

The total area covered by the construction phases of the building is unknown. What survives occupies much of the 625-square-meter area excavated by the Columbia University Expedition to Phlamoudhi. As no subsurface survey was conducted and parts of the site have either eroded or been cut away in more recent times, the extension of the building to the north, east, and west remains unknown as does what lay further south. From what survives, the largest form of the structure, in the thirteenth century BC, would probably have been at least 900 square meters, making it roughly the same size as Building X at Kalavasos-*Ayios Dhimitrios*. Long narrow storage halls, originally in the eastern part of the building and later in the southern and western parts of the building, contained large ceramic vessels called pithoi. When found, these vessels contained olives, almonds, figs (Dammann-Davis nd), possibly meats (Reese nd), and smaller vessels that might have served as scoops. Writing tools and inscriptions suggest that those contents were regulated, possibly because they were destined to feed people in the community. Based on what was uncovered, the purpose of the remainder of the building is unclear.

The building sat amid areas of ceramic, metallurgical, and oil production. From the scatters of ceramics in the area, it is assumed that there would have been residences, workshops, and other buildings around the *Melissa* structure. Whether there was a grid of streets or a city wall is unknown as is the extent of the inhabited area, although the size of the central building suggests that the *Melissa* site may have approached the more-than-ten-hectare size of some contemporary urban sites. Of particular note among the remains excavated is evidence for ceramic manufacture, for the large-scale storage of food and drink, for the introduction of new technologies in the later periods of occupation, and for increasing involvement in islandwide and international exchange.

Potters and early settlement

Even before the building at *Melissa* was constructed, people were working on the *Melissa* hill. A hole, two meters in diameter, first observed in Trench 11, was cut through the limestone bedrock and exposed to intense heat (fig. 9). Its size and the presence of failed ceramic vessels, or wasters, suggest strongly that this was a kiln. The wasters come mainly from large, handmade, Middle Bronze Age vessels formed with iron-rich clay that was tempered with fine sand to strengthen the walls of these sizable vessels. The vessels were covered with a fine slurry of the same clay that was brushed over the surface to form a thin slip. Although we do not know of the specific clay source used by these Bronze Age potters, the Columbia University Expedition to Phlamoudhi did identify clay sources and found evidence that pottery production continued in the area into the modern period.

One of the most recognizable wasters (fig. 10a) comes from the rim and neck of a Black Slip or Red Slip amphora, a large storage vessel for wine, water,

Fig. 9 View of *Melissa,* looking north

oil, or dry food. While both Black Slip and Red Slip vessels were made from the same red clay, their color was dependent on the flow of oxygen in the kiln. An oxidizing atmosphere allowed the iron-rich color of the clay to remain red. Reducing the oxygen created a carbon-rich atmosphere that turned the clay tan, brown, gray, or eventually black, depending on the length of time that the oxygen flow was reduced. Too high a temperature caused the vessels to vitrify. Initially, the vessels turned a yellowish-green color and their fabrics became brittle; these vessels are described as overfired. In some extreme instances, overfiring led to bubbling, slumping, and melting, resulting in vessels that we call wasters.

A vessel with a rim that is similar to the amphora waster is a large Black Slip amphora with a narrow neck from Phase 2. It has a reserved band with a wavy line pattern (fig. 10b). The pit for the kiln may have remained in use through Phase 2, after which it was covered over by a floor as part of an expansion of the building to

the south. To judge from vitrified vessels and lumps of unfired clay, ceramic production seems to have continued at *Melissa* into the later phases of the Bronze Age, but the location of later kilns is unknown.

The most notable feature of the pit carved out for the kiln is its size, which suggests that the careful monitoring of oxygen flow to the vessels being fired was a primary concern. How the size of the kiln would have been used to its greatest advantage is illustrated by another type of pottery made at *Melissa*. Typical of the northeastern coast of Cyprus and common at both *Melissa* and *Vounari* are vessels decorated with a red or black surface and red-painted decoration. At *Melissa* we find Red-on-Black vessels (figs. 11b–f, i) and Red-on-Red vessels (figs. 11g–h), as well as mistakes or experimental

Fig. 10 Ceramic waster and parts of a Black Slip II (Reserved Slip) amphora

pieces. The earliest of these pieces come from the deposits that predate the building (fig. 11a). Many of the Red-on-Black and other early vessels from *Melissa* were found in small pieces, due to the repeated building and rebuilding during the Bronze Age. A few early vessels are semicomplete because of their association with an early floor deposit or because a vessel was kept and used for many years after it was created.

To make a Red-on-Black vessel, the potter used iron-rich red clay tempered with various inclusions. Some potters favored tiny pieces of black sand, while most preferred pieces of crushed up pots, or grog. A few potters incorporated lime, but lime is problematic because it explodes out of the fabric if a vessel is fired at too high a temperature. To make a bowl, the potter is thought to have shaped a slab of clay over a rounded surface. With many Cypriot handmade vessels, the handles of jugs are rolls of clay that were punched through the bodies (figs. 11c–d). The exterior was smoothed over by adding another layer of clay to the handle and blending it with the vessel's body. Over the vessel, the potter spread a thick slurry of the same iron-rich clay used to build the vessel. That slipped surface was polished or burnished, giving the vessel a lustrous quality and sealing its pores. Jugs, bowls, and amphorae of Red-on-Black ware could hold liquid without leaking. Over the slip, the potters painted geometric patterns with the same clay slip. The process was laborious. Experiments with the polishing of a single pot show that it could take most of a day to complete.

The firing appears to have been similar to that used several centuries later for Greek Black- and Red-Figure vessels (Noble

Fig. 11 Red-on-Black and Red-on-Red vessels from *Melissa*

37

1988). First, the vessels were fired in an oxidizing atmosphere that left much of the fabric red. Second, the oxygen in the kiln was reduced, which blackened the surfaces of the vessels. A reintroduction of oxygen left the denser, polished, slipped surfaces black, while allowing the thinner and more porous slip-painted decorations to turn red again. In order to achieve an evenly Red-on-Black appearance, a kiln of about two meters in diameter would have been needed for consistent airflow. Experimental archaeological recreations of this process are currently under way by Polly Tessler.

Some potters at *Melissa* experimented with the building and decoration of the vessels. For example, a potter polished both the slipped surface and the paint in a streaky fashion on one piece (fig. 11a). An almost Black-on-Red appearance resulted because the painted decoration was denser than the areas covered only by a single layer of slip. Other pieces reveal how they were stacked in the kiln (fig. 11h): when the stacking impeded the air flow, the resulting firing blushes and lines of red or black created mottled appearances.

While most potters aimed to create Red-on-Black vessels, some appear to have intentionally fired vessels without reducing the oxygen in the kiln, leading to a Red-on-Red appearance (figs. 11g–h). Other pots are nearly vitrified, with the fabric darkened to a gray blue and the painted decoration becoming almost purple. Vessels include amphorae, large and small jugs, cups, and bowls with Red-on-Black and Red-on-Red patterns. The most common shape is a large bowl with a rounded bottom, with a rim diameter of thirty centimeters or more. Although their production may not have extended past the Late Cypriot I period, Red-on-Black and Red-on-Red vessels continued to be used at *Melissa* for hundreds of years. For example, two well-worn, round-bottomed jugs were found among vessels in the destruction of the Phase 6 building at the end of the thirteenth century BC (fig. 11i).

Red-on-Black and Red-on-Red vessels have been thought to be a product of northeastern Cyprus, where the majority of them have been found (Åström 1965). Until the discoveries at *Melissa,* the specific place of their origin was unknown. Whether *Melissa* was the only place of manufacture or just one of several remains to be determined. Chemical analyses planned for the future should

Fig. 12
Red-on-
Black and
Red-on-Red
wide platter
bowls from
Vounari

shed light on this matter. Elsewhere on Cyprus, Red-on-Black and Red-on-Red vessels appear at several sites south of the Kyrenia Mountains, but most come from Enkomi. This was the closest and largest growing urban center, located on the other side of the mountains from Phlamoudhi.

Bowls, cups, and jugs of Red-on-Black and Red-on-Red ware have also been found outside of Cyprus. They come mainly from places to the north and east of Cyprus, including Tarsus in Cilicia (ancient Kizzuwatna) just north of Phlamoud-hi, Alalakh along the Orontes River to the east, Ras Shamra on the Mediterranean coast of Syria, and coastal as well as inland Levantine sites such as Tell el-ʿAjjūl and Hazor. The vessels might have been shipped directly from the north coast or even via another Cypriot urban center such as Enkomi. That open shapes were exported shows that the vessels themselves were valued, not just what they might have contained. The lively decorations of Red-on-Black and Red-on-Red vessels may have made them desirable as exotica for display by wealthy elites both on and outside of the island.

The best evidence for the consumption of vessels made by potters at *Melis-sa* comes from the *Vounari* site. There, Red-on-Black, Red-on-Red (figs. 12–13),

39

Fig. 13 Red-
on-Black and
Red-on-Red
jugs, cups, and
amphorae from
Vounari

and other red-slipped vessels (fig. 16) were found, but the experimental pieces and mistakes characteristic of *Melissa* are missing. The *Vounari* examples are also better preserved, with larger pieces and more fragments of reconstructable vessels. At *Vounari*, we find several large bowls, some with large spouts, or platters (figs. 12a–b), suggesting that they were used for liquids or fine grains. Some of these bowls were broken and repaired in antiquity, an indication that they were valued even at a building so close to their place of manufacture (fig. 12c). Possibly a cessation in their production early in the Late Bronze Age increased their value. Jugs (figs. 13a–b), cups (figs. 13c–d), and amphorae (figs. 13e–g) complete the range of shapes used at *Vounari*.

Evidence for potters working at *Melissa* after Phase 2 is less clear, and there is no evidence for a kiln. Nevertheless, vitrified sherds continue to appear in fill deposits, as do lumps of unfired clay. Some vessels made in the red-slipped tradition, especially Base Ring II examples, appear to be variants or mistakes that are unlikely to have been used far beyond their place of manufacture.

Base Ring vessels (fig. 14), as the name implies, have a ring-shaped base. Some jugs in this shape are thought to have contained opium, which could be used medicinally or to induce a state of ecstasy (Merrillees 1962). Most examples from *Melissa* (Achilles nd) have a matte slip finish, a style often called Base Ring II. An earlier, finer, highly polished version, often called Base Ring I (fig. 14a), also occurs at *Melissa* in deposits predating Phase 5. No evidence suggests, however, that vessels of this fineware were made at *Melissa*.

Sarah Vaughan has shown that samples of Base Ring vessels from Phlamoudhi were made most likely of a local clay from the north, in the Lapithos formation called Kythrea Flysch (1991a). Base Ring II vessels were fired at temperatures between 750° and 850° C, which created a hard, metallic feel. Perhaps the imitation of metal was intentional, for many Base Ring shapes resemble the sharp lines characteristic of bronze vessels.

Most Base Ring vessels were fired in a reducing atmosphere, but often the firing was uneven, resulting in a blotchy surface. Some Base Ring II pots have white-painted decoration, as on a jug and pilgrim flask from *Melissa* (figs. 14c, e). A common Base Ring II form at *Melissa* is a bowl with a Y-shaped profile, which comes in two standard sizes, a small one with a rim diameter of about ten centimeters and a larger one with a rim diameter of about sixteen centimeters. Among the Y-shaped bowls are examples that appear to fit the general description of Base Ring II in addition to partly vitrified examples that show signs of melting

Fig. 14 Base Ring vessels from *Melissa*

Fig. 15 Red-slipped vessels from *Melissa*

and cracking. Some verge on collapse because the lower cup of the bowl has begun to sag and melt (fig. 14b). There are also softer, low-fired examples that resemble Black Slip and Red Slip wares (fig. 14d). Possibly because they were unsuitable as tablewares, several of the low-fired examples were adapted as lamps. On some bowls, the line where the wick burned remains on the rim and interior (fig. 14d).

Different kinds of vessels covered with red slip occur frequently throughout Bronze Age *Melissa*. Stacking lines continued to appear on Red Slip and Mono-chrome bowls (figs. 15b–c). A Red Slip jug of very soft fabric was found in a deposit between the Phase 4 and Phase 5 building (fig. 15a). Most of a Red Slip Wheelmade crater lay crushed on the floor of the Phase 6 building (fig. 15e). A Red Lustrous Wheelmade spindle bottle, a type of red-slipped pottery with particularly close parallels in Cilicia and the Hittite world of Anatolia, lay broken and spread across the floor of the Phase 6 building.

The red of north coast ceramics and the endurance of the red-slipped ceramic tradition there long after much of the island produced and used primarily white-ground vessels is of particular note in light of another craft from the area known for its rich red tones, namely textiles. Admittedly, our knowledge of the bright red textiles from the Karpass area, at which Phlamoudhi is just at the western edge, comes from historical periods (Papademitriou 1993: 9), but the geometric patterning on Red-on-Black and Red-on-Red ceramics may well reference textile patterns, as did geometric designs on vessels from other parts of the Mediterranean (Barber 1991: 365–72). Significantly, a mortar containing red pigment, possibly dye for woolen fibers, as well as several grinding tools were found on the floor of the Phase 6 building.

Food, drink, and storage

From its earliest period, *Melissa* served a community purpose. Even before the building went up, the kiln probably would have accommodated not just one but several potters, as is common even today (London et al. 1990). Potters' marks (fig. 15d) from the beginning of the site's occupation suggest that multiple potters marked their wares before bringing them to the hillside and placing them in a common kiln. As the kiln continued to be used and the building went up, a similar community purpose pervaded the place as it took on the central role of food and drink storage for those living at *Melissa* and in the area.

Fig. 16 Red-slipped vessels from *Vounari*

One of the primary functions of the *Melissa* building throughout its history was the storage of food and drink in large ceramic vessels called pithoi. In the thirteenth century BC on Cyprus, these vessels could be two meters in height (Keswani 1989; Pilides 2000). It is unlikely, however, that pithoi at *Melissa* were quite that large. The only nearly complete storage vessels, found on and set into the floor of the Phase 6 building, had bodies that were almost a meter in diameter, to judge from vessels that were found in the baulks, such as that between Trenches 4 and 22 (fig. 17). These vessels were likely at least a meter, if not a meter and a half, in height.

One pithos rim and neck, now lost, from the southern storage area of the site in Trench 10 bears an inscription in the undeciphered Cypro-Minoan script. Although its diameter was not recorded, the scale in the photograph shows that it was more than twenty-five centimeters in width and that the neck was approximately eighteen centimeters in height. Unfortunately, almost all the fragments of the reconstructable pithoi were left on site or in the schoolhouse in Phlamoudhi village.

Fig. 17 Late Cypriot IIC pithos from baulk between Trenches 4 and 22

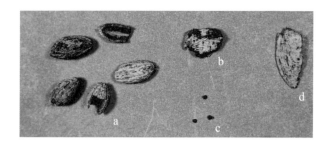

Fig. 18
Carbonized seed and fruit remains from
Trench 10 at *Melissa*

Nancy Dammann-Davis has studied the botanical remains from *Melissa*, including olive pits that were found inside one of the Phase 6 building pithoi. Her work shows that olives, figs, and almonds were stored in the vessels found on the floor of Trench 10 (fig. 18). Olives were a staple food at *Melissa* as well as across Cyprus and the Mediterranean. The olive fruits were probably pressed to make oil in Phases 5 and 6 of the building. In the areas where olive fruits were discovered, the burnt destructions of the building from Phases 5 and 6 were densely covered with ash, burnt mudbrick, and burnt vessels. Oil in storage would have contributed fuel for an intense fire. Also, in Trenches 12 and 24 just to the east, a pebbled surface that might be similar to that in the olive-pressing area at Kalavasos-*Ayios Dhimitrios* was uncovered for Phases 5 and 6 (fig. 9).

Cured meats and fish were also possibly stored in pithoi. David Reese, in his restudy of animal bone and shell finds from *Melissa*, has identified sheep/goat and bovine bones as well as crab and the remains of other marine creatures inside pithoi and in areas where Phase 6 pithoi were found. Animal bone and shell throughout the different building phases demonstrate that sheep/goat and cattle were butchered for meat and that people at Phlamoudhi also ate birds, marine fish, and shellfish, (figs. 19g–m). Earlier studies of animal bone from *Melissa* and *Vounari* identify the animals but do not relate the bone finds to the specific deposits at the sites (Hesse et al. 1975, 1983). Smaller vessels found inside the pithoi may furnish further evidence for the contents of the pithoi. One pithos in the baulk between Trenches 4 and 22 (fig. 17) contained a Base Ring II jug with a potmark on its handle, a Mycenaean chalice, and the lower portion or scoop of a wall bracket (fig. 20). Any of these vessels could have been used for dipping into the pithos. Alternatively, they simply might have fallen in during the collapse of the building.

Fig. 19
Shells
from
Vounari
and ani-
mal
bones
from
Melissa

Fig. 20
Vessels found inside
the pithos shown in
fig. 17

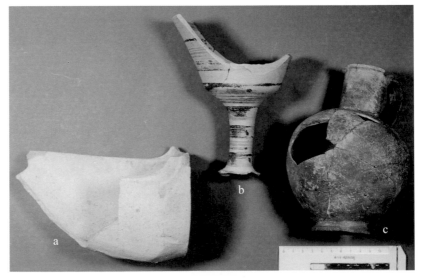

No specific evidence exists for the contents of pithoi before the Phase 6 building, but we do have many fragments of the vessels. For the first four building phases at *Melissa*, the fragments come primarily from two long corridor areas in Trenches 2, 5, 6, 7, 18, and 19 (fig. 21). The excavators kept only the most distinctive or diagnostic fragments, which are mainly pieces of vessel bodies that have horizontal and wavy bands of decoration.

Although we can not reconstruct the full shape and size of these vessels, the variety of fabrics and decorations tell us something about their significance. All are made from the iron-rich clay of Cyprus, but each potter added dif-

Fig. 21 View of the eastern side of the *Melissa* building, looking north

ferent inclusions to help support the weight of such large vessels. Gravel-sized lime (fig. 22a), sand (fig. 22b), and chaff (fig. 22c) represent just some of the ingredients used by the pithos makers. The surfaces are also treated variously. Some are plain (fig. 22e), others red slipped (fig. 22h), and others partly reduced for a white or tan surface color (figs. 22i–j).

The bands of decoration are equally diverse. Some were marked on a flat sur-

Fig. 22 Decorated pithoi from *Melissa*, Phases 1 through 4

face (figs. 22b, d, g), others on a distinctly raised band (figs. 22a, h–j), and still others have sculpted designs on an applied band (figs. 22c, e–f). It is noteworthy that applied bands of clay into which designs were set are particularly characteristic of the latest examples of these early pithoi. Such bands would have been the most easily seen and appear to be from thick-walled vessels that were likely more than a meter in height. Among the markings is one probably in the Cypro-Minoan script (fig. 22h), one of a small number of early inscriptions from the island. There are also several pieces marked with stamp seals, each of which is a multilobed or petaled circle (figs. 22g, 23b).

Significantly, similarly marked pithoi were found at *Vounari* in contemporary contexts (fig. 24). Even more remarkably, the same stamp seal was used to mark vessels at both *Melissa* and *Vounari* (figs. 23b, 24c), suggesting that the two places were linked administratively as well as by geography, view, and ceramic exchange. Markings such as these are found at other sites on Cyprus, particularly at Enkomi, where a similar lobed stamp seal was also used (Dikaios 1971: pl. 60.23). Although the practice of marking pithoi continued on Cyprus into the thirteenth century BC, at Phlamoudhi marked pithoi from later contexts (figs. 23a–b, d) appear to be fragments from earlier periods that ended up in fill deposits rather than vessels that were actually made in the fourteenth and thirteenth centuries BC. Some of these fragments from fill deposits are of interest for their figural content; one at *Melissa* appears to represent an olive branch (fig. 23d). At other sites, the marking involved the rolling of a stone cylinder seal or a larger wooden roller carved with figural decoration around a vessel (Webb and Frankel 1994), but none of these impressions was found at *Melissa*.

The markings on pithoi are probably linked to their makers or owners, for the bands of decoration would have been added before the vessels were fired. The markings may also be related to the contents of the vessels. For example, a study of seal-impressed oil containers from the site of Ebla in Syria suggests that the marks refer to quality, perhaps signifying different grades of oil (Mazzoni 1984). That the marks were meant to be seen is clear from their size

Fig. 23 Pithoi from *Melissa*, Phases 5 and 6

and prominent placement. Whether or not all the vessels at *Melissa* contained olives or oil in the early phases of the building is unknown, but it is likely that at least some did, given the later evidence from the site.

As the building began to be expanded beyond the two corridors where the early pithoi were found, the location, scale, and administration of storage began to change. By Phase 5, the horizontal expansion of the building clearly included a new storage area in the south (fig. 9). In Phase 6, that expansion continued toward the west (fig. 17) and seems also to have added a second story to the building, as suggested by part of a stair leading down into Trench 10 from the north.

The Phase 5 (fig. 23e) and 6 (figs. 23f–h) pithoi are larger and more similar in

Fig. 24 Decorated pithoi from *Vounari*

fabric and details of their manufacture than are those from the previous periods of occupation. Fewer potters were involved, possibly indicating that they began to specialize in the making of these much larger vessels. Whether fewer people were responsible for filling the pithoi is not known, but the lack of distinctive bands of decoration makes for the appearance of consolidated control over the vessels and their contents. Rather than the range of decorations that appear on the earlier vessels, Phase 5 and 6 pithoi all have finger-impressed wavy bands; any marking appears to be in the form of inscriptions added after the vessels were made.

The earlier decorated bands may have been supplanted by a new form of administration that involved written records on wax-filled writing boards. These could have been carried by administrators who could have written and erased text in the wax. Five bronze styli that would have been used to write on such boards were found in and among the destruction debris of the large storage area in the southern part of the site in Trench 10 and the baulk between Trenches 11 and 15 (fig. 25a). These tools have one pointed end for writing and one flattened end for erasing (Papasavvas 2003). Similar tools come from Late Bronze Age places where scribes wrote on waxed boards (Symington 1991), such as at the capital of the Hittites in central Anatolia.

A wooden board once filled with wax was found on board the ship that wrecked off the coast of Ulu Burun, Turkey, at the turn from the fourteenth to the thirteenth century BC (Payton 1991). Its trade route would have taken it right past Phlamoudhi. Taken together, the changes in storage and the changes in administration suggest that greater economic centralization and control accompanied greater social diversity at *Melissa*.

New technologies and expansion

New and enlarged industries accompanied the Phase 5 and 6 expansion of the *Melissa* building and its storage in the fourteenth and thirteenth centuries BC. Among these are metallurgy, textiles, and olive oil. Olive oil was probably already made at or near the *Melissa* site. But the pebbled area (fig. 9) added in Phase 5 to the east of the storage facility in the south may be evidence for the centralization of and possibly also an increase in oil production.

Direct evidence for textile manufacture is limited to terracotta spindle whorls (figs. 25g–j), which intact weigh between fifteen and thirty grams each. Spindle whorls attach to the end of a spindle stick, weighing it down as it spins fibers into thread. On Cyprus in the Bronze Age a spinner placed her whorl at the lower rather than the upper end of the spindle. Although men did spin, traditionally it was a woman's activity (Smith 2002a). There is evidence for spinning at *Melissa* around the time of the first building at the site (fig. 25g). Spindle whorls continue to appear in deposits from Phases 2 through 4 (fig. 25h) but are most common during Phases 5 and 6 (figs. 25i–j). The whorls at *Melissa* would have been suitable for spinning light and medium weight fibers, possibly wool. The number of sheep bones found at *Melissa* attest to a readily available source of wool. No loom weights or other weaving tools were discovered. The grinding stones and the mortar with red pigment (now lost) from the floor of Phase 6, however, might have been used for preparing dyes to color the wool.

The most noticeable technological change at *Melissa* during Phases 5 and 6, however, is in metallurgy. The only metal from a deposit earlier than the fourteenth century BC is an amorphous lump whose purpose is unknown. Evidence for metalwork is limited to the melting of bronze, rather than the primary smelt-

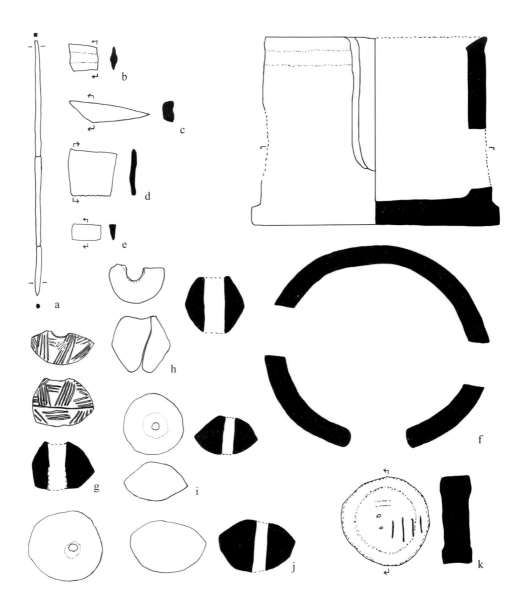

Fig. 25 Stylus, bronze fragments, possible bellows, and terracotta spindle whorls from *Melissa;* lead weight from *Vounari*

ing of copper ore. A vessel containing metal from Phase 5, probably a crucible, is now lost. Waste materials, called slag, come mainly from Phase 6, in parts of Trenches 10, 11, and 12. This slag is full of copper staining and wood. Also from Phase 6 is a cylindrical ceramic vessel, which was thought by the excavators to be the model of a house (fig. 25f). Found overturned amid the debris from the Phase 6 building destruction between Trenches 10 and 11, it might have formed part of a bellows to keep coals burning if it were fitted with ceramic tubes, or tuyères, in its two side holes and a loose skin were affixed around the ridges at the top.

Other than the bronze writing tools, all objects of that metal are preserved only in small fragments that were deliberately cut. One can still make out parts of a dagger, spear, saw, and axe blade (figs. 25b–e), but these were no longer used as weapons or tools; instead they would have been valued by weight (Kroll 2003) and may have been intended to be recycled into new objects. The metal fragments were strewn on the floors of the Phase 5 and 6 southern storage areas. Along with the Phase 6 pieces were found weights appropriate for measuring out small amounts of metal as well as sheets of lead. Possibly these sheets were meant to be melted along with the bronze in the recycling of the metals.

Islandwide and international contacts

During the long history of *Melissa*, a certain amount of contact occurred with people and places in other parts of Cyprus and overseas. Their nearest neighbors at *Vounari* and along the north coast appear to have been culturally most similar to them. Even though Red-on-Black and Red-on-Red ceramics and other products from the north coast were used by people elsewhere during the first several centuries of the Bronze Age at Phlamoudhi, the inhabitants of *Melissa* and its environs seem to have adopted little if anything from other cultures into their daily life. This pattern changed in the fourteenth century BC, when the *Melissa* building was expanded significantly to the south and the west. Not only was metallurgy added to the craft specializations centered there, but the inhabitants of *Melissa* also began to adopt luxuries, symbols, and hospitality customs common to other parts of Cyprus and the eastern Mediterranean.

Foremost among the cultural changes was the adoption of some white-ground ceramic vessels for serving, eating, and drinking (figs. 26–27). After centuries of using largely locally made, red-slipped dining sets, inhabitants of *Melissa* added Aegean, specifically Mycenaean, and Aegean-style cups and jugs to their pantries. Almost all of these vessels were found crushed on the floors of the Phase 6 building. Across the Mediterranean, an increasing taste for vessels made in the Aegean took hold, particularly in the fourteenth and thirteenth centuries BC. Shared preferences for dining and serving vessels suggest shared traditions of hospitality and feasting among people who traveled, or hosted those who traveled, across land and sea. Many used ceramics originally made in the Mycenaean world of Greece; still others used locally made cups, plates, jugs, and craters that resembled Mycenaean-style vessels.

The inhabitants of *Melissa* imported oil containers or dispensers as well as some tableware. One imported shape is the stirrup jar, which has a spout and two handles that curve down as if forming stirrups on either side of a central knob. A large, coarse Late Minoan IIIA example from Crete would have contained olive oil (fig. 26d); a small, fine, and lustrous Mycenaean IIIA2 example from the Greek mainland probably contained perfumed oil (fig. 26a). A small Mycenaean IIIA2 cup and beaked jug (figs. 26b–c) also form part of the assemblage. Most remarkable is the Mycenaean style chalice (fig. 20b) found inside a Phase 6 pithos (Yon et al. 2000: 61–62).

More common are so-called White Painted Wheelmade III vessels, which are painted red, brown, or dark brown on a light ground. Unlike their Mycenaean counterparts, the surfaces are matte. There are bowls (figs. 27a–b) and cups (fig. 27c) as well as a mixing crater (fig. 27g), probably for wine, and another crater (fig. 27h). A small closed jar called an alabastron (fig. 27d) and several feeder juglets (figs. 27e–f) were probably used for containing and dispensing small amounts of oil. Numerous vessels used as lamps were found near these pieces in the southern storeroom, suggesting that oil dispensers and lamps were on hand to bring light into this part of the building.

White-ground vessels were not unknown at Phlamoudhi before the later periods of the Bronze Age. For example, White Painted and Bichrome vessels from Cyprus and the Levant (fig. 28) date back to the early periods of the *Melis-*

Fig. 26
Aegean-
imported
vessels
from
Melissa

Fig. 27
White
Painted
Wheel-
made ves-
sels from
Melissa

sa building's construction. Similar pieces were found at *Vounari* (fig. 29). Most notable among these is a large Bichrome crater (fig. 28g) from the debris of the Phase 6 building in Trench 25 and the baulk between Trenches 22 and 25, found together with a plainware platter measuring more than thirty centimeters in diameter. Also of note is a painted White Shaved jug from Phase 6 (fig. 28h). Among the light-ground vessels from *Melissa* are pieces that represent animals. One Middle Bronze Age zoomorphic hollow pouring vessel called an askos (fig. 28j) and a small White Painted jar or amphora that depicts the spotted hide of an animal, possibly a bull (fig. 28i), come from surface deposits.

A distinct category of white-ground vessels is called White Slip, a Cypriot product that was used from the Near East across to the western Mediterranean. Like the Red-on-Black and Red-on-Red vessels, they were valued not only as containers but as objects in themselves. White Slip bowls and jugs have a lustrous sheen and lively geometric patterns, making them attractive for display. These vessels have an iron-rich, coarse clay core covered by a thick, smooth, and polished white slip that did not contain iron and thus retained its white color no matter what the oxygen content of the firing conditions was (Aloupi et al. 2001).

Fig. 28
White Painted and Bichrome vessels from *Melissa*

Over the white surface are patterns painted with a slurry of iron-rich clay and later with manganese, the color of which was also not altered by changes in oxygen during firing. The vessels were fired at temperatures exceeding 1000° C.

Small numbers of White Slip sherds date back as early as the Phase 2 building at *Melissa*. The earliest piece is Proto White Slip (fig. 30a) and there are also several White Slip I and Bichrome examples (figs. 30b–d, f). Most fragments are White Slip II, generally considered to be the latest style of White Slip, with a particularly well preserved so-called milk bowl (fig. 30e), or round-bottomed bowl, from the Phase 6 destruction debris. Scholars still debate the appropriateness of the term "milk bowl" and whether the vessels were for yogurt.

Fig. 29 White Painted, Bichrome, White Slip, Aegean-style, and Tell el-Yahudieh ware vessels from *Vounari*

Significantly, well-preserved White Slip I and II vessels were found together in the debris of the Phase 6 building, suggesting that bowls (figs. 30d–e) and small craters (fig. 30f) were kept and used over a long period of time. Other fragments appear to have been covered originally with White Slip (fig. 30g), which did not adhere well to the vessel walls. Similar products occur elsewhere on Cyprus, including Sanida-*Moutti tou Aghiou Serkou*, a White Slip production center north of Kalavasos-*Ayios Dhimitrios* (Todd and Pilides 2001: 39–40). It is probable that all these White Slip pieces are imports to *Melissa* from the southern

Fig. 30
White Slip vessels from *Melissa*

part of Cyprus. They, like the heirloom Red-on-Black and Red-on-Red vessels from earlier days, remained in use over many centuries.

In addition to accumulating dining and serving sets that conformed with Mediterranean-wide traditions of hospitality, people at Phlamoudhi began to have access to luxury materials for furniture and personal adornment. Among the remains of items stored in the southern part of the building were tiny fragments of objects, possibly furniture, inlaid with ivory and covered with gold. An early indication of the availability of luxury personal items are the carnelian and glass beads that were strewn on the Phase 4 floor of the southern part of the building. The cylinder seal (fig. 4) mentioned in the introduction may belong with those pieces, but its context was mixed and it could have still been in use during the thirteenth century BC.

Even stone grinders and tools furnish evidence of access to imported stones and prestige items. For example, vesicular basalt from the Sea of Galilee region was used for a large grinding platter that broke and was covered over before the Phase 6 building. An unfinished mace head from the Phase 6 destruction could have been intended as a weapon or a symbol of a person's powerful political or religious role at or near the site.

The *Melissa* site was destroyed by fire sometime around 1200 BC. The original kiln had long ago been covered over, surfaced with a lime plaster floor, and forgotten. But the floor created a problem for those who used the *Melissa* building. As time went by, water ran through the subsurface limestone, gradually widening and making the original hole deeper. The floor sagged and was resurfaced repeatedly. Ultimately, a wall was built along the edge of the original hole and a large pithos was placed on the floor. With the burnt destruction, probable earthquakes, and ultimate collapse of the Phase 6 building, the pithos fell through the floor, pulling down the wall and the other objects on the floor with it. The pit, originally thought by the excavators to be a tomb, turned out to reveal the productivity of *Melissa* and the original organization of the community. Although it was not built as a tomb, it entombed parts of the last Late Bronze Age building until the place was rediscovered centuries later in the Iron Age.

Phlamoudhi-Vounari

Phlamoudhi-*Vounari* is contemporary mainly with Phases 1 through 4 at *Melissa*, as well as *Melissa*'s preconstruction activity. The earliest object from *Vounari* is a single Red Polished ware sherd from a fill deposit that predates *Vounari*'s Phase 3 (fig. 16a). Apart from this sherd, which may have been brought to the site as part of mudbrick building material, nothing suggests that the *Vounari* site predates the *Melissa* settlement. The structure at *Vounari* was built and rebuilt at least ten times from the time of its initial construction in the Middle Cypriot III period and the abandonment of the site, probably in the Late Cypriot IIA period (Al-Radi 1983 with revisions by Horowitz nd) (fig. 31). Its construction falls into five major phases, some of which have several refloorings, as well as a period of limited use with considerable erosion.

Phase 1 (shadow phase)	Early–Middle Bronze Age
Phase 2 (first building)	Middle Cypriot III–Late Cypriot IA
Phase 3 (3 periods)	Late Cypriot IB–Late Cypriot IIA
Phase 4 (4a–f)	Late Cypriot IIA
Phase 5 (north gate built)	Late Cypriot IIA
Phase 6	Erosion of Bronze Age site

The monumental building

Vounari is a conical hill that rises about ten meters above the surrounding fields. The excavated area of approximately nine hundred square meters included the entire mound. At its maximum size, the building filled almost that entire space, making it about the same size as the large building at *Melissa*. No evidence for Bronze Age activity was found in surveys around the mound, indicating that *Vounari* stood alone in the second millennium BC. From *Vounari* one can see up the mountain pass to the south, out to sea to the north, west to the *Melissa* settlement, and east, possibly to other as-yet-unlocated Bronze Age sites in that direction. Its visibility was an important part of its role in the region (fig. 32).

A report on *Vounari* was published by Selma Al-Radi in 1983, in which she proposed that *Vounari* was a sanctuary. Current work by Mara Horowitz, encompassing both the full range of ceramics from the site as well as small finds and architecture, emphasizes that the imposing monumental building on the mound would have been a focal point in the landscape. Some cult activity may have taken place at *Vounari*, as suggested by possible altars and pits with traces of burning found inside the buildings. Its primary significance, however, was most likely as a storage and transport station.

Vounari might have been involved in shipping, using anchorages off the seacoast. There were several seashells from *Vounari* (figs. 19a–f) as there were at *Melissa,* but thus far there is no evidence for a permanent harbor nearby. Overland trade would have been equally, if not more, important. As a node along a trade route, some cult activity would not have been out of place. The sea could be treacherous; the Kyrenia Mountains are steep, and the crossing may not always have been easy. Significantly, on the south side of the mountain is a small cult site at Ayios Jakovos-*Dhima* (Gjerstad et al. 1934).

After some initial use of the hilltop, where there are traces of burning, the first building was constructed. With walls more than a meter thick, the building might have exceeded one story. An exterior feature thought to have been an altar with an adjacent ash pit was disturbed in the Iron Age, so its significance remains uncertain. Red-on-Black and Red-on-Red pottery from Phase 2 suggests some connections with *Melissa* at this early point.

Subsequent construction in Phases 3 and 4 includes several rebuildings and refloorings (fig. 33). The Phase 3 building is characterized by a monumental stone platform, with a wall or bench lining the south side. Much of this phase,

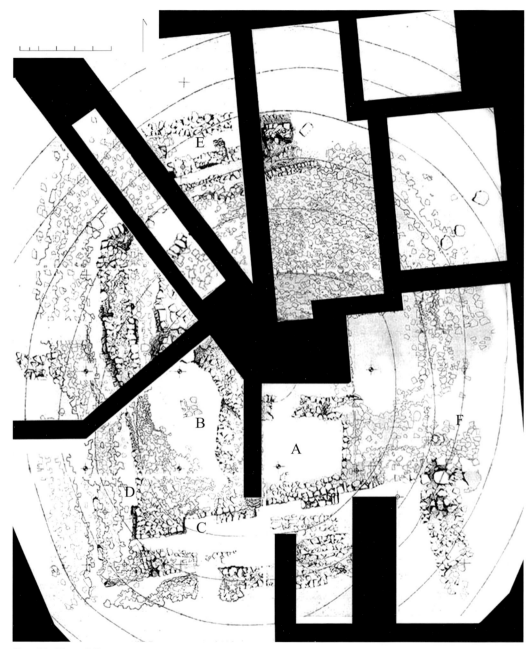

Fig. 31 Plan of *Vounari*

Fig. 32 View looking east from *Melissa* to *Vounari*

however, was disturbed by later rebuildings of the site, and no trace of the building that stood atop the platform survives. In Phase 4, buttresses were added to
support the platform, and a wall surrounded the platform creating a corridor. In
Phase 5 a new entrance that faced north and a ramp or stair in the southeast were
built. Around the exterior wall was plaster that Mara Horowitz has identified as a
series of working floors, rather than as a decorative facing around the building. It
is here and in the corridor that much of the pottery from the site was found, in
connection with floor deposits rather than rubble fill. Although the appearance of
the upper portions of this or earlier forms of the building is unknown, part of it
was used for storage pithoi. The ramp suggests that there was an effort to widen
access and ease the flow of people, possibly animals, and products in and out of
the building.

Fig. 33 View of the southwest corner of *Vounari*

Pots, pithoi, and accounting

Vounari compares closely with *Melissa* in most details of its ceramic assemblage. People at *Vounari* seem to have obtained Red-on-Black and Red-on-Red cups, bowls, jugs, and amphorae from *Melissa* (figs. 12–13). *Vounari* might even have served as a transfer point in the distribution of these pots to other parts of Cyprus or to places north and east. As at *Melissa*, such pots and other early red-slipped ceramics (fig. 16b) continue to have been used at *Vounari* for many years after their creation. Several older pots were reused as lamps, among them a fine Monochrome bowl with a loop handle (fig. 16f), a Red-on-Red bowl with a double-pronged handle (fig. 16g), and a Base Ring I ware cup (fig. 16d). A few Red Lustrous Wheelmade and Base Ring II fragments attest to the latest periods of use in *Vounari* (figs. 16c, e), possibly even into the Late Cypriot IIB period of the middle fourteenth century BC.

A similar chronology exists for other fineware ceramics from *Vounari*. White Painted (figs. 29a–b, d–f) and Bichrome (fig. 29g) ceramics from Cyprus and the Levant as well as White Slip I (figs. 29h–i) and White Slip II (fig. 29j) vessels compare well with pieces from *Melissa*. They also might support an early Late Cypriot IIB date for the final use of *Vounari*. The only fragment with a possible Egyptian connection found in the Phlamoudhi excavations appears to be one Middle Bronze Age Tell el-Yahudieh ware sherd (fig. 29c). A few Mycenaean and locally made Mycenaean-style fragments (figs. 29k–m) come from post–Bronze Age deposits at *Vounari* but are too fragmentary to be firm chronological indicators.

Decorated pithoi comparable with those from *Melissa* first appear in association with the Phase 3 platform and continue through the remaining history of the site (fig. 24). We do not know what was stored in these pithoi, but presumably they contained goods for long-distance as well as local exchange, including oils and other foods, ceramics, and even perishable products. Similar decorations, including the use of the same stamp seal at both *Melissa* and *Vounari*, provide support for an administrative link between the two places.

Among the few nonceramic finds from *Vounari* are a lead weight (fig. 25k), a piece of folded lead, and fragments of bronze, which bolster the argument that *Vounari* was a place for trade. The weight is circular and bears two dots and four vertical marks that, if read in a western decimal or a Near Eastern sexigesimal system, signify the number 24. The piece weighs in at 255 grams, making it the equivalent of 24 standard units of a measurement (approximately 10.63 grams) that is common to Cyprus, the Levant, and the Hittite world (Courtois 1983). The folded lead piece and bronze fragments are reminiscent of similar pieces of metal from *Melissa* that may have been intended to be melted down and recycled.

Trade routes and abandonment

Why *Vounari* was abandoned long before the settlement at *Melissa* was destroyed probably had something to do with the expansion of the *Melissa* site and changes in its social and economic interests. The abandonment of *Vounari* coincides with the end of other small sites in the foothills of the Kyrenia Mountains and in the

Karpass Peninsula. For example, the small sanctuary at Ayios Jakovos-*Dhima* goes out of use by the end of the Late Cypriot IIA period. Nitovikla, an isolated tower or fortification, along the south coast of the Karpass Peninsula goes out of use at about the same time (Hult 1992). Although somewhat larger than *Vounari*, Nitovikla may have served a similar function, given the many marked pithoi found there. Enkomi, which began its history with a fortification structure that also contained similarly decorated pithoi, grew and changed into a sprawling urban place.

Possibly the shift away from sites such as *Vounari* and Nitovikla signaled a change in trading patterns. *Vounari* was active as part of a trade route when the larger *Melissa* was involved primarily in the economic and social activities of the north coast. By the fourteenth century BC, *Melissa* began to participate in Mediterranean-wide traditions. Further, if potters there engaged in Base Ring ceramic manufacture as proposed, the clays for those vessels have been identified west of *Melissa*. An interest in another urban center known for ceramic production, Toumba tou Skourou (Vermeule and Wolsky 1990), may also have contributed to that shift. A new pattern of travel in that direction still would have allowed *Melissa* to look to the sea as well as south to Enkomi, for a river route from a pass near Akanthou leads to that urban center. That route, however, would not have run through *Vounari*. To be sure, metallurgy became important at both *Melissa* and *Vounari*. The scrap metal suitable for recycling, however, does not indicate that copper came directly from the Troodos Mountains. Even so, in shifting their trade pattern, travelers to and from *Melissa* may have adapted to the system of river routes used as common avenues of exchange to and from other urban centers on the island.

III. CYPRUS IN THE FIRST MILLENNIUM BC

After the growth of large urban centers such as Kition and Kouklia at the end of the Bronze Age, Cyprus once again was marked by a series of separate urban areas, only this time they were in addition to the large centers that took hold at the end of the Bronze Age. Called city-kingdoms, several are known through excavations and ancient documents. Texts list different numbers of kingdoms at different points in time. For example, an eighth-century-BC stele set up on behalf of the Assyrian king Sargon II lists seven kingdoms on Cyprus. A seventh-century inscription from the time of Esarhaddon lists ten.

Several languages and writing systems were in use on Cyprus. The Cypro-Syllabic script reads as Greek in many cases. Still other examples appear to reflect a local, as yet unreadable, language of Cyprus. Both the Phoenician and the Greek alphabets also came to be used on the island. During the first millennium BC, Cyprus vacillated and fragmented under the influence or control of the Phoenicians, Assyrians, Egyptians, Persians, Greeks, and ultimately the Ptolemies of Egypt.

Salamis replaced Enkomi as the center on the east coast. Kourion grew at the base of the Kouris River, along which Alassa and Episkopi-*Bamboula* once held sway. Paphos, the home of the sanctuary of Aphrodite, continued to thrive. By the Classical period, the Phoenicians were powerful not only at Kition but also at Idalion, Tamassos, and Amathus.

Attempts have been made to divide up the Iron Age Cypriot landscape to fit the number of known kingdoms (Rupp 1989), allocating space to those mentioned above as well as to Soloi, Marion, Chytroi, Ledra, and Lapithos. These, however, represent only hypothetical boundaries. Survey and excavation evidence suggests that boundaries were marked by liminal spaces such as sanctuaries (Given 1991; Bazemore 2002; Given and Smith 2003) and that not all territory was subsumed under the aegis of the rulers. Lands of the living, the dead, and the gods integrated to shape the character of each city kingdom.

Until recently, very little was known about the physical cities before the Classical period. Increasing evidence from places such as Idalion (Hadjicosti

1997), Amathus (Aupert 1996), and Marion (Childs 1997) is filling in that picture with palaces, archives, and smaller residences. We are also learning how sanctuaries formed integral parts not only of cultic but also the economic and social landscapes of the island (Smith 1997). They were places of worship as well as centers of craft, economic, and probably political activity.

While our understanding of the first millennium BC has become richer, particularly for the Archaic, Classical, and Hellenistic periods, our knowledge of the Cypro-Geometric period, which links the Bronze Age with the later periods, is sparse. For that period, we have mainly the remains of tombs. Man, woman, or child, wealthy or poor—evidence for them all can be found in funerary spaces. By observing how the living honored the dead, we can learn how some of the wealthy split from the centers that were prominent at the end of the Bronze Age and established new places of power that grew into the kingdoms known from later periods.

Settlement and sanctuary in Phlamoudhi

Whether Phlamoudhi formed part of one of the city kingdoms mentioned in texts is unknown. It lies near the hypothetical border between Chytroi (Kythrea) and Salamis (near ancient Enkomi) (Rupp 1989: 347), which cuts indiscriminately across the Kyrenia Mountains but is still instructive. Just as Phlamoudhi in the Bronze Age might have been part of a trade route eastward and over the mountains to Enkomi, it might also have been part of a different route westward and through a mountain pass to access resources available in the direction of Kythrea.

The Bronze Age buildings at *Melissa* and *Vounari* had been long buried by the time that they were rediscovered. At *Melissa,* remains of a Cypro-Archaic to Cypro-Classical period structure with a finely faced southern side and door and pivot stone to the west was found built over part of Trench 4 and extending just into Trenches 10 and 14. Although there were no floors, in the topsoil and at the tops of the walls were fragments of a large lamp (fig. 34a), a bowl (fig. 34b), a stemmed drinking cup (fig. 34c), a circular handle of a bronze bowl (fig. 34e), a small amphora (fig. 34f), a pithos (fig. 34g), and a transport amphora (fig. 41f), among other vessels. Additionally, a piece of painted terracotta (fig. 34d) appears

Fig. 34 Cypro-Archaic and Cypro-Classical finds from *Melissa*

to be part of an architectural decoration, perhaps from this building. If so, it suggests that the building was more than a plastered mudbrick structure.

Farther west, above the remains of the Bronze Age storage area, was an Archaic period terracotta male figurine with a pointed cap that was either part of a horse-and-rider votive or may have represented a musician (fig. 35a). Just west of where he was found, in Trench 11, a construction of four ashlar blocks at the end of a wall built at a right angle appears to form another part of an Archaic to Classical period, or even a Hellenistic, structure. Later terracing and erosion stripped away any floors of these buildings.

Down the slope, to the north in Area B Trench 1, a number of Classical period, mold-made, terracotta female figurines (fig. 35e, g) were found amid the mudbrick remains of a building with Classical and Hellenistic pottery in it (fig. 41a). Originally, several of the figurines probably held their arms out as part of a ring dance. One Archaic period terracotta model of a tree might once have been placed at the center of such a dance (fig. 35f). An Archaic period Egyptianizing male head also comes from the debris (fig. 35d).

The exact plans of the Archaic, Classical, and Hellenistic buildings are unclear. Among the objects found at *Melissa*, however, there are votives that support the interpretation of parts of the place as a sanctuary as well as vessels suited for eating, drinking, display, and storage. Some remains of metallurgical activity that postdates the Bronze Age were found near the male figurine with the pointed hat and suggest that workshops may have been located nearby.

At *Vounari* we find additional evidence for a lively Archaic, Classical, Hellenistic, and, even possibly, a Geometric period site (fig. 36). On the north side of the mound, people rebuilt over the Bronze Age ramp, erected a wall to the west, and ultimately dug a pit in which they buried figural votives and pottery vessels. Surveys around the mound suggest that the area was also inhabited at this time.

An amphora with a latticed lozenge design on its neck may date to the Cypro-Geometric period, although it could also be from the Archaic period (fig.

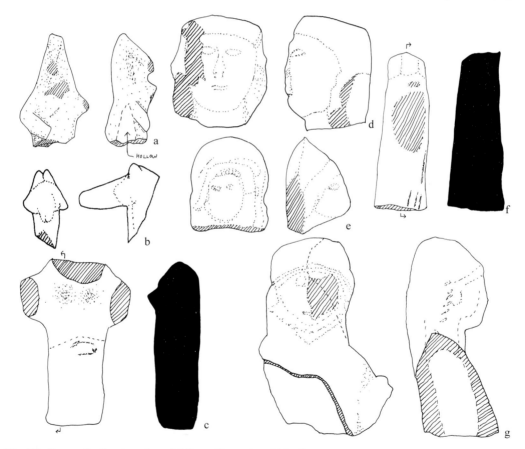

Fig. 35 Terracotta figurines from *Melissa*, *Vounari*, and *Marikou*

Fig. 36
Cypro-
Geometric
to Cypro-
Classical
ceramics
from
Vounari

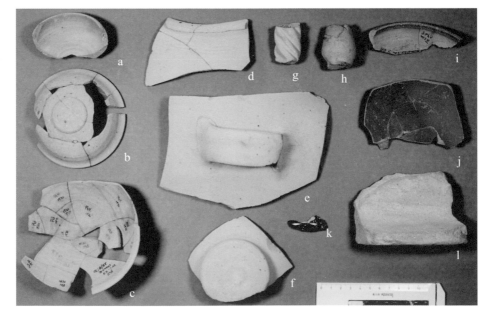

Fig. 37
Late Clas-
sical and
Hellenistic
ceramics
from
Vounari

36a). Another amphora with concentric circles (fig. 36f), a jug with pinched rim (fig. 36b), and other juglets and jugs (figs. 36c–d, k), probably used for the storage and pouring of food, are firm evidence that the site was used in the Cypro-Archaic II period. Lamp fragments also come from this period (figs. 36i–j). A fragment of a bell with a hole for the clapper (fig. 36e) along with a terracotta figurine of a horse are the best evidence for the placement of Archaic period votives at the site (fig. 35b).

Transport and other storage vessels from the late Archaic or Classical and Hellenistic periods (figs. 36g–h, 37d–f) indicate that food was brought into the sanctuary. Late Classical and Hellenistic

Fig. 38 Near-life-size male statue discovered at *Vounari* in 1970

ceramics from *Vounari*—jugs (fig. 37g) as well as cups and plates (figs. 37a–c, i–j) for eating, drinking, or the placement of dedications—continued at the site for several centuries. Roof tiles (fig. 37l) from the mound appear to postdate the Hellenistic period, so the roofing structure of the building at *Vounari* is unknown. Very little from this period appears to be imported. One black glazed sherd (fig. 37k) is a Greek product. A miniature votive jug (fig. 37h), limestone statuettes, and a striking, near-life-size, robed male statue carrying a staff (fig. 38) are some of the votives dedicated in the sanctuary. This statue, found at the top of the mound, was one of the first items uncovered.

The cult places at *Vounari* and *Melissa* both reuse Bronze Age architecture, a common practice across Cyprus, which also occurs in other parts of the

Mediterranean at this time. Possibly places associated with a legendary past were preferred. What particular deities were worshipped is not entirely clear, as no inscription tells us his or her name. The votives that people chose to stand in for themselves as worshippers give some idea of who might have been worshipped. The horse-and-rider figurines would be appropriate for Apollo, and his cult was well known on the island, particularly at Kourion (Buitron-Oliver 1996). Another sanctuary found in a field called *Marikou* turned up an Archaic period female figurine with upraised arms (fig. 35c), in addition to figurines similar to the mold-made examples from *Melissa*. She as well as other female figurines would have been appropriate dedications to the goddess of Cyprus, whose main temple was in Paphos.

Resting places of the dead in Phlamoudhi

Continuing a practice begun in the Bronze Age, chamber tombs were the standard form of burial. With one or more chambers carved into the rock or soil to accommodate members of extended families, a single tomb can provide a view into generations of a family. Tombs contain human remains, jewelry, and burial shrouds, as well as furniture and tablewares to accompany the dead into the next world; lamps, jugs, bowls, and other equipment used by the living to honor the dead, to light their visits to the chambers, and to perfume the air are also found.

Two tombs excavated by the Columbia University Expedition to Phlamoudhi are typical of other tombs discovered in their survey. One was a late Archaic to early Classical chamber tomb at *Pallouri*, just north of *Melissa* (fig. 5). No human remains survived, but there were plates, lamps, jugs, and a trumpet shell. The tomb at *Spilios tou Tsali* (fig. 6) is a Hellenistic rock-cut tomb similar to the well-known Tombs of the Kings in Paphos. Carved into the limestone, the tomb preserves architectural details such as columns, engaged columns, moldings, and roofing. It was probably the resting place of wealthy residents of the Phlamoudhi area.

How these sanctuaries and tombs fit into the settled landscape along the north coast of Cyprus in the first millennium BC remains to be determined. The sanctuaries could have been at the edges of settled areas, or they could have been at the center of economic and craft spaces. The survey evidence around *Vounari* and the possibility of a decorated building at *Melissa* suggest that neither had a sanctuary that stood apart from a settlement. These remains are tantalizing evidence that rather than being simply at the limits of the known city kingdoms of Salamis and Chytroi, *Melissa* and *Vounari* might have been vibrant parts of a previously undocumented Iron Age landscape.

IV. CYPRUS IN THE FIRST AND SECOND MILLENNIA AD

Roman, Byzantine, Medieval, Ottoman, and Modern Cyprus are rich with their own histories of interconnections among places east, west, north, and south. Under the Romans, Cyprus saw great prosperity. Her cities and temples flourished. In mosaics preserved in the houses of the wealthy at Paphos, Kourion, and Salamis, we can observe the change in worship from Greek and Roman gods to Christianity. For example, ancient heroes such as Heracles are pictured in scenes that foreshadow depictions of the infant Christ (Daszewski and Michaelides 1988: 62–63). The church of Cyprus had already been established firmly by the time of Constantine the Great in the fourth century AD.

Toward the end of the Late Roman period, a series of Arab raids weakened the island. The Byzantine period saw the rebuilding of Cyprus as part of the Eastern Empire; church buildings from this period still stand today, some with colorful frescoes covering the walls, in local styles as well as the style of Constantinople.

In the Medieval period, the Latin Church was established on the island. Cyprus changed hands many times, from Richard the Lionheart to the Frankish kings of Jerusalem to the Venetians. This history of the island's forming first part of one empire and then the next slowed while it was under the rule of the Ottomans, which lasted for more than three hundred years until Cyprus became part of the British Empire. In 1960, the island became the independent Republic of Cyprus, which became divided politically in 1974 and remains divided today.

Phlamoudhi in the Roman Period

From the Columbia survey and from the excavated sites of *Melissa* and *Vounari*, Roman period remains are almost entirely limited to ceramics found on the surface or in topsoil deposits. They were kept for their diagnostic features and do not represent the great range of undecorated ceramics from the period. Trenches 21 and 23 in the southwestern part of the *Melissa* site produced several Roman period ceramic and glass sherds as well as a bronze coin, identified by Kyle Killian as a piece dated to AD 408–423 from the reign of Theodosius II (AD 408–450). The head of the emperor is on the reverse with two standing emperors on the obverse. Architectural remains in Trenches 21 and 23 were not associated with anything

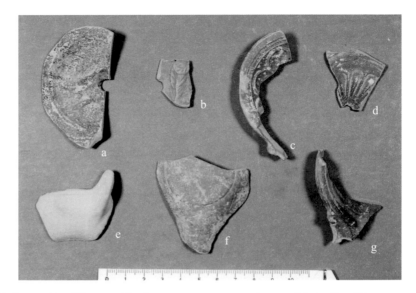

Fig. 39
Roman lamps from
Vounari

other than topsoil deposits. The walls, however, appear to postdate the Bronze Age structures; they are wider and could well be Roman in date.

The ceramics that remain from *Melissa* and *Vounari* indicate that most were made locally, with the exception of a range of well-preserved lamps from the first through third century AD (fig. 39) found at *Vounari*, which form part of Kyle Killian's study of the Roman pottery from Phlamoudhi. These include several with molded figural decorations: a bird (fig. 39a), a possible image of Venus (fig. 39b), and floral motifs (figs. 39c–d). Locally made lamps also come from *Vounari* (fig. 39e) and *Melissa* (fig. 41c).

Among the Roman vessels are several first-century-BC redware plates, which are local products (figs. 40b, 41g) and imported terra sigillata (fig. 40a). A small amphora (fig. 41b) and cooking vessels (fig. 41h) come from *Melissa* and are not diagnostic of a particular century during the Roman period. Several glass fragments were recorded (fig. 40e), but

Fig. 40 Roman and later sherds from *Vounari*

few survive today. From the preserved remains it appears that *Melissa* has the more likely evidence for Roman period settlement, whereas *Vounari* might well have continued to function as a special purpose place, possibly continuing as a hilltop sanctuary.

Phlamoudhi in the Byzantine and Medieval Periods

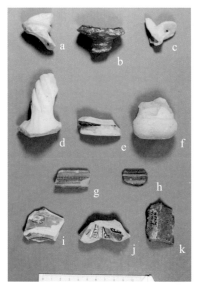

Fig. 41 Late Classical and Hellenistic through Medieval pottery from *Melissa*

There is a small church at *Melissa*. Not much was recorded about it by the excavators, but its presence is important because the ancestors of the inhabitants of the village of Phlamoudhi had previously lived near the *Melissa* site. Sophocles Hadjisavvas lists it as a recent structure (1991: 11), but possibly there had been a church building there much earlier, for he also notes the presence of a Byzantine settlement at *Melissa*. The church continued its life even after the settlement was moved to the current village of Phlamoudhi. Sgrafitto-ware pottery (fig. 41j) also attests to Byzantine activity at *Melissa*.

A bronze coin from *Vounari,* identified by Kyle Killian as a piece issued during the reign of Manuel I (1143–1180), comes from nearly the end of the Byzantine period. It depicts the Virgin and Child on one side and Manuel I on the other. Particularly well preserved Byzantine and later glazed wares (figs. 40c–d, g–i) also come from *Vounari*, but less is known about the function of that place during these later periods until the settlement of the village of Phlamoudhi. Using that village as its base, the Columbia University Expedition sought to collect archaeological information about the area. With that they began to reconstruct the prehistoric and historic past of this coastal strip north of the Kyrenia Mountains of Cyprus.

LIST OF FIGURES

77

21. South of Trenches 14, 10, 11, and 12 respectively are Trenches 20, 13, 15, and 16. West of Trenches 1+1-3+3, 4, and 14 respectively are Trenches 25, 22, and 23. East of Trenches 7 and 12 respectively are Trenches 9 and 24. North of Trenches 1+1-3+3, 2, and 7 respectively are Trenches 17, 18, and 19. Area B Trench 1 lies twenty meters north of Trench 17. Area B Trench 2 lies five meters north of Trench 19. (map by Angel Coronado, Columbia University Expedition to Phlamoudhi map archive)

9   View of *Melissa,* looking north. Trench 11 with the pit feature is in the foreground. To the right and running north are the early storage areas of Phases 1 to 4, to the far right is part of the pebbled surface in Trench 12, and to the left and far left running north are the expanded parts of the building with later period storage areas of Phases 5 and 6. (Columbia University Expedition to Phlamoudhi slide archive)

10   (a) Ceramic waster (T19.44.2) from the rim of an amphora predating the Phase 1 building, (b) parts of a Black Slip II (Reserved Slip) amphora (made of fragments from T2.18, T2.20, T5.11, T5.12, T5.13, and T5.18) from Phase 2 at *Melissa*. Scale 1:4. (photograph by J. S. Smith, Phlamoudhi Archaeological Project photo archive)

11   Red-on-Black and Red-on-Red vessels from *Melissa*. (a) Bowl (T7.41.1), (b) bowl spout (T2.22.123), (c) jug handle (T6.12.3), (d) jug handle (T2.13.31), (e) jug body (T19.39.1), (f) jug body and handle (T5.14.1), (g) bowl or cup rim and loop handle (T2.14.86), (h) bowl (T2.5.1), (i) round-bottomed jug (Pit.23.2). Scale 1:4. (photograph by J. S. Smith, Phlamoudhi Archaeological Project photo archive)

12   Red-on-Black and Red-on-Red wide platter bowls from *Vounari*. (a) Spout (WB1.18.2), (b) spouted bowl (S2a–h several batches), (c) bowl with repair holes (N11.3.1). Scale 1:4. (photograph by J. S. Smith, Phlamoudhi Archaeological Project photo archive)

13   Red-on-Black and Red-on-Red jugs, cups, and amphorae from *Vounari*. (a) Jug neck and handle (S2 Batch 3), (b) jug neck (E2 GL Batch 1), (c) cup rim and handle (S2 Batch 2), (d) cup rim and base (S2 a–h Batch 30), (e) amphora rim and neck (SB1.6.1), (f) amphora rim and neck (SB1.6.22), (g) amphora handle and body (N9.4.1). Scale 1:4. (photograph by J. S. Smith, Phlamoudhi Archaeological Project photo archive)

14   Base Ring vessels from *Melissa*. (a) Bowl with ridged decoration (T2.7.3), (b) Y-shaped bowl (T3.6.10), (c) painted jug neck and shoulder (T10.21.2), (d) Y-shaped bowl (T10.13.31), (e) painted pilgrim flask body (Pit.24.1). Scale 1:4. (photograph by J. S. Smith, Phlamoudhi Archaeological Project photo archive)

15   Red-slipped vessels from *Melissa*. (a) Red Slip jug (T2.8.26), (b) Red Slip bowl rim (T2.31.1), (c) Monochrome bowl rim and handle (T5.5.11), (d) Red Slip handle with potmark (T7.29.21), (3) Red Slip Wheelmade amphora rim, neck, and shoulder (made of fragments from T1–3.1 and T1–3.4). Scale 1:4. (photograph by J. S. Smith, Phlamoudhi Archaeological Project photo archive)

16   Red-slipped vessels from *Vounari*. (a) Red Polished sherd (S3a/b 27/8/70 Batch 2), (b) Red Slip jug (SB1.6.23), (c) Red Lustrous bowl rim (N10.4.8), (d) Base Ring I bowl rim (WB1.7.1), (e) Base Ring II bowl rim (WB1.X.1), (f) Monochrome bowl with loop handle (W4.3.1), (g) Red-on-Red bowl with pronged handle (WN1.1). Scale: 1:4. (photograph by J. S. Smith, Phlamoudhi Archaeological Project photo archive)

17   Late Cypriot IIC pithos found in the baulk between Trenches 4 and 22 in 1973 at *Melissa*. Holly Pittman looks inside where the vessels in fig. 20 were found. (Columbia University Expedition to Phlamoudhi slide archive)

18   Carbonized plant remains from burnt debris in and among Phase 6 pithoi in Trench 10 at *Melissa*. (a) Olive pits (T10.21), (b) fleshy part of a fig (T10.22), (c) fig seeds (T10.22), and (d) almond (T10.21). Scale 1:1. (photograph by J. S. Smith, Phlamoudhi Archaeological Project photo archive)

19   Shells from *Vounari* and animal bones from *Melissa*. (a) Euthria cornea (Ph W1), (b) Cerithium vulgatum (Ph V), (c) Patella (Ph Ger), (d) Murex trunculus (Ph V S), (e) Luria lurida (N7a.2(1)), (f) Charonia (EB1.1), (g–h) sheep/goat molars (T5.5 [C]), (i) cattle shaft cut down in butchering (T5.5 [T]), (j) sheep/goat rib, cut from vertebra in butchering (T5.5 [H]), (k) large marine fish spine fragment (T5.5 [H]), (l–m) sheep/goal vertebrae cut through in butchering (T5.5 [H]). Scale 1:2. (photograph by J. S. Smith, Phlamoudhi Archaeological Project photo archive)

20   Vessels from Locus 4, found inside pithos from the baulk between Trenches 4 and 22 (see fig. 17). (a) Lower scoop of a terracotta wall bracket (inv. no. 73.3.66), (b) Mycenaean chalice (inv. no. 73.3.65), (c) Base Ring II jug with potmark on upper handle (inv. no. 73.3.64). Scale 1:4. (photograph by J. S. Smith, Phlamoudhi Archaeological Project photo archive)

21   View of the eastern side of the *Melissa* building, looking north. Trench 5 is in the foreground, and Sally Dunham is standing in Trench 2. Phases 2 through 4 building walls can be seen.

22   Decorated pithoi from *Melissa*, Phases 1 through 4. Phase 1 deposit: (a) T19.31.2; Phase 2 deposits: (b) T5.6.8, (c) T5.6; Phase 3 deposits: (d) T2.16.67+T4.21.41, (e) T19.40.4, (f) T7.48.18; Phase 4 deposits: (g) T18.7.19, (h) T5.5.121, (i) T4.2.34, (j) T7.3.1. Scale 1:4. (photograph by J. S. Smith, Phlamoudhi Archaeological Project photo archive)

23   Pithoi from *Melissa*, Phases 5 and 6. Phase 5 deposits: (a) T7.5.14, (b) T1.19.35, (c) T3.13.19; Phase 5–6 deposits: (e) T1.19.1+T1.12.1; Phase 6 deposits: (d) B22-25.3.4, (f-g) T1–3.3.1, (h) T1.15.1. Scale 1:4. (photograph by J. S. Smith, Phlamoudhi Archaeological Project photo archive)

24   Decorated pithoi from *Vounari*. (a) N10.8.10, (b) N8-N8a.19.1, (c) NB3.1.3, (d) N11.3.11, (e) S3b.1–9FF.6, (f) SB1.6.81, (g) W4.4.4, (h) N10.4.5. Scale 1:4. (photograph by J. S. Smith, Phlamoudhi Archaeological Project photo archive)

25   Stylus, bronze fragments, possible bellows, and terracotta spindle whorls from *Melissa* as well as

a lead weight from *Vounari*. All are at a scale of 1:2 except the bellows, which is 1:4. (a) Bronze writing stylus (inv. no. 73.3.48b), (b) dagger fragment (T10.27), (c) spear tip (inv. no. 73.3.16), (d) saw blade (inv. no. 73.3.3), (e) axe blade (inv. no. 73.3.61), (f) possible ceramic bellows (inv. no. 73.3.40), (g) incised biconical spindle whorl (inv. no. 73.3.29), (h) biconical spindle whorl (inv. no. 71.3.37), (i) burnt biconical spindle whorl (inv. no. 73.3.22), (j) polished biconical spindle whorl (inv. no. 73.3.67), (k) numerically marked lead weight (inv. no. 70.1.8). (drawings by J. S. Smith, Phlamoudhi Archaeological Project drawing archive)

26 Aegean imported vessels from *Melissa*. (a) Small Mycenaean stirrup jar (B10–14.10.4), (b) Mycenaean cup (BX.11.10), (c) spouted Mycenaean juglet (B11-15.39.2), (d) Minoan coarseware stirrup jar (T14.16.7). Scale 1:4. (photograph by J. S. Smith, Phlamoudhi Archaeological Project photo archive)

27 White Painted Wheelmade vessels from *Melissa*. (a) Bowl (T11.40.1), (b) bowl (B10–11.4.11), (c) cup (T11.37.31), (d) alabastron shoulder (BX.7.5), (e) feeder jug spout (T10.20.2), (f) feeder jug body, base, and handle (T10.18.66), (g) crater rim and body (T10.19.1), (h) crater body (T10.14.1). Scale 1:4. (photograph by J. S. Smith, Phlamoudhi Archaeological Project photo archive)

28 Bichrome and White Painted vessels from *Melissa*. Bichrome: (a) T5.6.60, (b) T4.21.111, (c) B22-25.3.17, (g) B22-25.1.1+B22-25.4+B22-25.3+T25.3; White Painted: (d) T5.16.10, (e) T5.6.63, (f) T5.5.118, (i) TT2.99.8, (j) Area B T2.18.1; White Shaved: (h) T10.21.9. Scale 1:4. (photograph by J. S. Smith, Phlamoudhi Archaeological Project photo archive)

29 White Painted, Bichrome, White Slip, Aegean-style, and Tell el-Yahudieh ware vessels from *Vounari*. White Painted: (a) S2a–h.39, (b) N10.6.15, WB3.1.2, S2c.3.1, (d) N9.4, (e) N9.3, (f) SB1.6; Bichrome: (g) W3a.0; White Slip: (h) S2c.8+SS/SSa.2, (i) N10.6, (j) W4.3.3; Mycenaean: (k) N8a.8, (l) N8a.2(1a); White Painted Wheelmade: (m) NB3.1; Tell el-Yahudieh: (c) S2.S8 AH 1970. Scale 1:4. (photograph by J. S. Smith, Phlamoudhi Archaeological Project photo archive)

30 White Slip vessels from *Melissa*. (a) T2.18.1, (b) T5.2.58, (c) T4.21.13, (d) Sq2.2.1+T4.2.14, (e) B10-11.3.1, (f) T10.21.10, (g) T10.19.12. Scale 1:4. (photograph by J. S. Smith, Phlamoudhi Archaeological Project photo archive)

31 Plan of *Vounari*. Trenches were arranged according to north (N), south (S), east (E), and west (W) and labeled numerically in sequence (1, 2, 3, etc.) as they were excavated. Baulks between trenches were recorded by adding a "B" after the trench designation (for example, WB for baulks in the western part of the mound). The earliest structure (A) and its possible altar (B), which was disturbed by Iron Age activity, the platforms with Phase 4 buttresses (C) and corridor with exterior wall (D), as well as the northern entrance area that was reused in the Iron Age structure (E), and the southeastern stair or ramp (F), are all visible on the plan. (plan by Angel Coronado, Columbia University Expedition to Phlamoudhi map archive)

32   View looking east from *Melissa* to *Vounari*, which is visible as the small light-colored mound in the center of the photograph. Both sites lie in the two-kilometer-wide stretch of arable land between the Mediterranean Sea (to the left) and the Kyrenia Mountain range (to the right).

33   View of the southwest corner of *Vounari,* showing platforms, buttresses, and walls. (Columbia University Expedition to Phlamoudhi photo archive)

34   Cypro-Archaic and Cypro-Classical finds from *Melissa*. (a) Lamp (T4.2.10), (b) Black-on-Red hemispherical bowl rim (T4.2.18), (c) Bichrome stemmed bowl (T4.1.11), (d) painted architectural terracotta (T10.1.46), (e) bronze handle (T4.2), (f) White Painted amphora neck and rim (T14.1.37), (g) pithos (T4.2). Scale 1:4. (photograph by J. S. Smith, Phlamoudhi Archaeological Project photo archive)

35   Terracotta figurines from *Melissa*, *Vounari*, and *Marikou*. *Melissa*: (a) handmade, hollow male (73.3.24), (d) limestone male (72.3.17), (e) mold-made, solid female (72.3.25), (f) handmade, solid tree (72.3.15), (g) mold-made, hollow female (72.3.18); *Vounari*: (b) handmade, solid horse (73.1.6); *Marikou*: (c) handmade, solid female (*Marikou* 6). Scale 1:4. (Drawings by J. S. Smith, Phlamoudhi Archaeological Project drawing archive)

36   Cypro-Geometric to Cypro-Classical ceramics from *Vounari*. (a) White Painted amphora rim and neck (N9.3/1.22), (b) White Painted trefoil jug (S3(0) 20/8/70 Batch 2), (c) plain juglet (NB1.1.14), (d) double-rolled jug handle (NB1.X.1), (e) bell handle and clapper hole (N6.1.1), (f) Bichrome amphora body (N8.6.1(12)), (g) pithoid amphora handle (N8a1–1a.2), (h) pithoid amphora base (N10.1.9), (i) trefoil lamp (W3-A(0)2+4), (j) trefoil lamp nozzle (SB1.1.B22), (k) cooking jug (N10.4.5). Scale 1:4. (photograph by J. S. Smith, Phlamoudhi Archaeological Project photo archive)

37   Late Classical and Hellenistic ceramics from *Vounari*. (a) Inturned-rim bowl (WB1.1.5), (b) bowl (W1/W2), (c) bowl (PhV 1970), (d) hole-mouth jar rim (N8a.2.1), (e) amphora handle (N7a.2(1).4), (f) amphora base (N6a.1.1), (g) twisted handle (EB1.1.4), (h) votive juglet (W1 1970), (i) two-tone slip bowl (W1.X.4(1a)), (j) painted and dipped bowl (PhV 1970), (k) Greek black glaze (N6a(1)), (l) roof cover tile (SE.X.7). Scale 1:4. (photograph by J. S. Smith, Phlamoudhi Archaeological Project photo archive)

38   Near-life-size male statue (inv. no. 70.1.1+70.1.2) discovered at *Vounari* in 1970. Selma Al-Radi stands behind the statue.

39   Roman lamps from *Vounari*. (a) Imported, bird on a branch (PhV 14/8/70 W1), (b) imported, Venus (N7a(0)), (c) imported, floral (PhV(St) W1 14/8/70), (d) imported, floral (PhV(St) 14/8/70), (e) local lamp base (NB1.1), (f) imported lamp base (PhV(St) 14/8/70), (g) imported lamp spout (PhV). Scale 1:2. (photograph by J. S. Smith, Phlamoudhi Archaeological Project photo archive)

40   Roman and later sherds from *Vounari*. (a) Terra sigillata plate (PhV 14/8/70), (b) Cypriot sigillata plate (W1-S3 baulk 28/8/70), (c) green glaze rim (WB2.1), (d) slip-painted ware (W3A(0).3+4 +

W4.1 + W3.0 + N8.0), (e) folded glass rim (PhV), (f) lid (WB.1), (g–i) glazed wares. Scale 1:4. (photograph by J. S. Smith, Phlamoudhi Archaeological Project photo archive)

41   Late Classical and Hellenistic through Medieval pottery from *Melissa*. (a) High ring foot (Area B T1.11.1), (b) amphora toe (Area B T1.7.6), (c) lamp handle (Area B T1.3.28), (d) spiral handle (BX.2.2), (e) dipped, drip base (T10.2.45), (f) amphora toe (B14-20.2.1), (g) red-slipped rim (T1.6.30), (h) cooking ware rim (T1.6.34), (i) red-slipped plate base (T23.1.73), (j) sgrafitto base with incised decoration, possibly showing a person's clothing (T6.1.23), (k) glazed ware handle (T16.1.1). Scale 1:4. (photograph by J. S. Smith, Phlamoudhi Archaeological Project photo archive)

Back cover: View of Phlamoudhi-*Vounari*, looking north (Columbia University Expedition to Phlamoudhi slide archive)

BIBLIOGRAPHY

Achilles, D. nd. "Base Ring Ware (from Phlamoudhi-*Melissa*)." Unpublished paper.

Aloupi, E., V. Perdikatsis, and A. Lekka 2001. "Assessment of the White Slip Classification Scheme Based on Physico-Chemical Aspects of the Technique," 15–26, in V. Karageorghis ed., *The White Slip Ware of Late Bronze Age Cyprus*. Vienna: Österreichischen Akademie der Wissenschaften.

Al-Radi, S. M. S. 1983. *Phlamoudhi Vounari: A Sanctuary Site in Cyprus* (Studies in Mediterranean Archaeology 65). Göteborg: Paul Åströms.

Artzy, M., I. Perlman, and F. Asaro 1976. "Alasiya of the Amarna Letters," *Journal of Near Eastern Studies* 35: 171–82.

Åström, P. 1965. "Red-on-Black Ware," *Opuscula Atheniensia* 5: 59–88.

———— 1989. *Hala Sultan Tekke 9: Trenches 1972–1987, with an Index for Volumes 1–9* (Studies in Mediterranean Archaeology 45:9). Göteborg: Paul Åströms.

Aupert, P., ed. 1996. *Guide d'Amathonte*. Athens: École française d'Athènes.

Barber, E. J. W. 1991. *Prehistoric Textiles: The Development of Cloth in the Neolithic and Bronze Ages with Special Reference to the Aegean*. Princeton: Princeton University Press.

Bazemore, G. B. 2002. "The Display and Viewing of the Syllabic Inscriptions of Rantidi Sanctuary," 155–212, in J. S. Smith ed., *Script and Seal Use on Cyprus in the Bronze and Iron Ages* (Colloquia and Conference Papers 4). Boston: Archaeological Institute of America.

Benson, J. L. 1956. "Aegean and Near Eastern Seal Impressions from Cyprus," 59–70, in S. S. Weinberg ed., *The Aegean and the Near East, Studies Presented to Hetty Goldman on the Occasion of Her Seventy-fifth Birthday*. Locust Valley, NY: J. J. Augustin.

———— 1972. *Bamboula at Kourion: The Necropolis and the Finds*. Philadelphia: University of Pennsylvania Press.

Buitron-Oliver, D. 1996. *The Sanctuary of Apollo Hylates at Kourion: Excavations in the Archaic Precinct* (Studies in Mediterranean Archaeology 109). Jonsered: Paul Åströms.

Cadogan, G. 1989. "Maroni and the Monuments," 43–51, in E. Peltenberg ed., *Early Society in Cyprus*. Edinburgh: Edinburgh University Press.

Catling, H. W. 1962. "Patterns of Settlement in Bronze Age Cyprus," *Opuscula Atheniensia* 4: 129–69.

Childs, W. A. P. 1997. "The Iron Age Kingdom of Marion," *Bulletin of the American Schools of Oriental Research* 308: 37–48.

Courtois, J.-C. 1983. "Le trésor de poids de Kalavassos-Ayios Dhimitrios 1982," *Report of the Department of Antiquities, Cyprus*: 117–30.

Courtois, J.-C., J. Lagarce, and E. Lagarce 1986. *Enkomi et le bronze récent à Chypre*. Nicosia: A. G. Leventis Foundation.

Dammann-Davis, N. nd. "Archaeobotanical Investigation of the Late Bronze Age Site, Phlamoudhi-*Melissa,* Cyprus." Unpublished paper.

Daszewski, W. A., and D. Michaelides 1988. *Guide to the Paphos Mosaics*. Nicosia: Bank of Cyprus Cultural Foundation.

Dikaios, P. 1969, 1971. *Enkomi: Excavations 1948–1958*. 3 vols. Mainz am Rhein: Philipp von Zabern.

du Plat Taylor, J. 1952. "A Late Bronze Age Settlement at Apliki, Cyprus," *The Antiquaries Journal* 32: 133–67.

Given, M. 1991. "Symbols, Power, and the Construction of Identity in the City-Kingdoms of Ancient Cyprus ca. 750–312 BC." Ph.D. diss., Cambridge University.

Given, M., and A. B. Knapp 2001. "Troodos Archaeological and Environmental Survey Project: First Preliminary Report (June–July 2000)," *Report of the Department of Antiquities, Cyprus*: 425–40.

———— 2003. *The Sydney Cyprus Survey Project: Social Approaches to Regional Archaeological Survey* (Monumenta Archaeologica 21). Los Angeles: Cotsen Institute of Archaeology, University of California, Los Angeles.

Given, M., and J. S. Smith 2003. "Geometric to Classical Landscapes," 270–77, in Given and Knapp 2003.

Gjerstad, E., J. Lindros, E. Sjöquist, and A. Westholm 1934. *The Swedish Cyprus Expedition Volume I: Finds and Results of the Excavations in Cyprus 1927–1931*. Stockholm: The Swedish Cyprus Expedition.

Goodwin, J. C. 1984. *An Historical Toponymy of Cyprus*. Nicosia: Privately published.

Goren, Y., S. Bunimovitz, I. Finkelstein, and N. Na'aman 2003. "The Location of Alashiya: New Evidence from Petrographic Investigation of Alashiyan Tablets from El-Amarna and Ugarit," *American Journal of Archaeology* 107: 233–55.

Hadjicosti, M. 1997. "The Kingdom of Idalion in the Light of New Evidence," *Bulletin of the American Schools of Oriental Research* 308: 49–63.

Hadjisavvas, S. 1989. "A Late Cypriot Community at Alassa," 32–42, in E. Peltenberg ed., *Early Society in Cyprus*. Edinburgh: Edinburgh University Press.

———— 1991. *Καταβολές I: Αρχαιολογική Ερισκόπηση 20 Κατεχομένων Σήμερα Χωριών της Επαρχίας Αμμοχώστου*. Nicosia: Department of Antiquities of Cyprus.

———— 2001. "Seal Impressed Pithos Fragments from Alassa: Some Preliminary Thoughts," 61–67, in P. M. Fischer ed., *Contributions to the Archaeology and History of the Bronze and Iron Ages in the Eastern Mediterranean: Studies in Honour of Paul Åström*. Vienna: Österreichisches Archäologisches Institut.

———— 2003. *From Ishtar to Aphrodite: 3200 Years of Cypriot Hellenism: Treasures from the Museums of Cyprus*. New York: Alexander S. Onassis Public Benefit Foundation (USA).

Hesse, B., A. Ogilvy, and P. Wapnish 1975. "The Fauna of Phlamoudhi-*Melissa*: An Interim Report," *Report of the Department of Antiquities, Cyprus*: 5–28.

――― 1983. "Report on the Fauna from Phlamoudhi Vounari," 116–18, in Al-Radi 1983.

Hogarth, D. G. 1889. *Devia Cypria*. London: H. Frowde.

Horowitz, M. nd. "Phlamoudhi *Vounari*: New Perspectives on a Multi-Function Site." Unpublished paper.

Hult, G. 1992. *Nitovikla Reconsidered* (Medelhavsmuseet, Memoir 8). Stockholm: Medelhavsmuseet.

Karageorghis, V., and M. Demas 1985. *Excavations at Kition Volume V: The Pre-Phoenician Levels, Areas I and II*. Nicosia: Department of Antiquities of Cyprus.

Karageorghis, V., and V. Kassianidou 1999. "Metalworking and Recycling in Late Bronze Age Cyprus–the Evidence from Kition," *Oxford Journal of Archaeology* 18: 171–88.

Karageorghis, V., G. S. Merker, and J. R. Mertens 2004. *The Cesnola Collection: Terracottas*. New York: Metropolitan Museum of Art.

Keswani, P. S. 1989. "The Pithoi and Other Plain Ware Vessels," 12–21, in South et al. 1989.

――― 1996. "Hierarchies, Heterarchies, and Urbanization Processes: The View from Bronze Age Cyprus," *Journal of Mediterranean Archaeology* 9: 211–50.

Killian, K. nd. "The Hellenistic, Roman and Medieval Material from Phlamoudhi." Unpublished paper.

Kling, B., and J. D. Muhly nd. "Joan DuPlat Taylor's Excavations at the Late Bronze Age Mining Settlement at Apliki-*Karamallos*, Cyprus." Unpublished manuscript.

Knapp, A. B. 1997. *The Archaeology of Late Bronze Age Cypriot Society: The Study of Settlement, Survey and Landscape*. Glasgow: University of Glasgow, Department of Archaeology.

――― ed. 1996. *Sources for the History of Cyprus Volume II: Near Eastern and Aegean Texts from the Third to the First Millennia B.C.* Altamont, NY: Greece and Cyprus Research Center.

Knapp, A. B., and J. F. Cherry 1994. *Provenience Studies and Bronze Age Cyprus: Production, Exchange and Politico-Economic Change* (Monographs in World Archaeology 21). Madison, WI: Prehistory Press.

Knapp, A. B., V. Kassianidou, and M. Donnelly 2001. "Excavations at Politiko *Phorades* and the Archaeology of Ancient Cypriot Copper Mining," *Near Eastern Archaeology* 64: 202–8.

Kroll, J. H. 2003. "Weights, Bullion, Currency, Coinage," 313–23, in N. Stampolides and V. Karageorghis eds., *ΠΛΟΕΣ . . . Sea Routes . . . Interconnections in the Mediterranean: 16th–6th c. B.C.: Proceedings of the International Symposium held at Rethymnon, Crete, September 29th–October 2nd 2002*. Athens: University of Crete and the A.G. Leventis Foundation.

London, G. A., F. Egoumenidou, and V. Karageorghis 1990. *Traditional Pottery of Cyprus*. Mainz: Philipp von Zabern.

Maier, F. G. 1975. "The Temple of Aphrodite at Old Paphos," *Report of the Department of Antiquities, Cyprus*: 69–80.

Maier, F. G., and V. Karageorghis 1984. *Paphos: History and Archaeology*. Nicosia: A. G. Leventis Foundation.

Manning, S. W., D. A. Sewell, and E. Herscher 2002. "Late Cypriot IA Maritime Trade in Action: Underwater Survey at Maroni-Tsaroukkas and the Contemporary East Mediterranean Trading System," *Annual of the British School at Athens* 97: 97–162.

Mazzoni, S. 1984. "Seal Impressions on Jars from Ebla in EB I A-B," *Akkadica* 37: 18–40.

Merrillees, R. S. 1962. "Opium Trade in the Bronze Age Levant," *Antiquity* 36: 287–92.

———— 1984. "Ambelikou-Aletri: A Preliminary Report," *Report of the Department of Antiquities, Cyprus*: 1–13.

———— 1992. "The Government of Cyprus in the Late Bronze Age," 310–28, in P. Åström ed., *Acta Cypria: Acts of an International Congress on Cypriote Archaeology held in Göteborg on 22–24 August 1991, part 3* (Studies in Mediterranean Archaeology Pocket-book 120). Jonsered: Paul Åströms.

Murray, A. S., A. H. Smith, and H. B. Walters 1900. *Excavations in Cyprus*. London: British Museum.

Myres, J. 1914. *Handbook of the Cesnola Collection of Antiquities from Cyprus*. New York: Metropolitan Museum of Art.

Noble, J. V. 1988. *The Techniques of Painted Attic Pottery*. New York: Thames and Hudson.

Palaima, T. G. 1989. "Cypro-Minoan Scripts: Problems of Historical Context," 121–87, in Y. Duhoux, T. G. Palaima, and J. Bennet eds., *Problems in Decipherment* (Bibliothèque des Cahiers de l'Institut de Linguistique de Louvain 49). Louvain-la-neuve: Peeters.

Papademitriou, E. 1993. *Cyprus Folk Art: Exhibition Organised on the Occasion of the Commonwealth Heads of Government Meeting Cyprus 21–25 October 1993*. Nicosia: Cultural Services, Ministry of Education and Culture.

Papasavvas, G. 2003. "Writing on Cyprus: Some Silent Witnesses," *Report of the Department of Antiquities, Cyprus:* 79–94.

Payton, R. 1991. "The Ulu Burun Writing-Board Set," *Anatolian Studies* 41: 99–106.

Pilides, D. 2000. *Pithoi of the Late Bronze Age in Cyprus: Types from Major Sites of the Period*. Nicosia: Department of Antiquities of Cyprus.

Pittman, H. 1995. "Edith Porada, 1912–1994," *American Journal of Archaeology* 99: 143–46.

Porada, E. 1948a. *Corpus of Ancient Near Eastern Seals in North American Collections. Volume I: The Collection of the Pierpont Morgan Library* (Bollingen Series 14). New York: Pantheon.

———— 1948b. "The Cylinder Seals of the Late Cypriote Bronze Age," *American Journal of Archaeology* 52: 178–98.

———— 1986. "Late Cypriote Cylinder Seals Between East and West," 289–99, in V. Karageorghis ed., *Acts of the International Archaeological Symposium "Cyprus Between the Orient and the Occident," Nicosia, 8–14 September 1985*. Nicosia: Department of Antiquities.

Pulak, C. 2001. "The Cargo of the Ulu Burun Ship and Evidence for Trade with the Aegean," 13–60, in L. Bonfante and V. Karageorghis eds., *Italy and Cyprus in Antiquity: 1500–450 BC*. Nicosia: Costakis and Leto Severis Foundation.

Reese, D. nd. "Phlamoudhi-*Melissa* fauna." Unpublished paper.

Rupp, D. 1989. "Puttin' on the Ritz: Manifestations of High Status in Iron Age Cyprus," 336–62, in E. Peltenberg ed., *Early Society in Cyprus*. Edinburgh: Edinburgh University Press.

Schaeffer, C. F. A. 1952. *Enkomi-Alasia I: Nouvelle Missions en Chypre 1946–1950*. Paris: C. Klincksieck.

——— ed. 1971. *Alasia I*. Paris: C. Klincksieck.

Smith, J. S. 1997. "Preliminary Comments on a Rural Cypro-Archaic Sanctuary in Polis-*Peristeries*," *Bulletin of the American Schools of Oriental Research* 308: 77–98.

——— 2002a. "Changes in the Workplace: Women and Textile Production on Late Bronze Age Cyprus," 281–312, in D. Bolger and N. Serwint eds., *Engendering Aphrodite: Women and Society in Ancient Cyprus* (American Schools of Oriental Research Archaeological Reports 7, Cyprus American Archaeological Research Institute Monographs 3). Boston: American Schools of Oriental Research.

——— 2002b. "Problems and Prospects in the Study of Script and Seal Use on Cyprus in the Bronze and Iron Ages," 1–47, in J. S. Smith ed., *Script and Seal Use on Cyprus in the Bronze and Iron Ages* (Archaeological Institute of America Colloquia and Conference Papers Series 4). Boston: Archaeological Institute of America.

——— 2003. "Writing Styles in Clay of the Eastern Mediterranean Late Bronze Age," 277–89, in N. Stampolides and V. Karageorghis eds., *ΠΛΟΕΣ...Sea Routes . . . Interconnections in the Mediterranean: 16th–6th c. B.C.: Proceedings of the International Symposium held at Rethymnon, Crete, September 29th–October 2nd 2002*. Athens: University of Crete and the A.G. Leventis Foundation.

Sørensen, L. W., and D. W. Rupp eds. 1983. *The Land of the Paphian Aphrodite 2* (Studies in Mediterranean Archaeology 104:2). Göteborg: Paul Åströms.

South, A. 1989. "From Copper to Kingship: Aspects of Bronze Age Society Viewed from the Vasilikos Valley," 315–24, in E. Peltenberg ed., *Early Society in Cyprus*. Edinburgh: Edinburgh University Press.

——— 1992. "Kalavasos-Ayios Dhimitrios 1991," *Report of the Department of Antiquities, Cyprus*: 133–46.

South, A., P. Russell, and P. S. Keswani 1989. *Kalavasos-Ayios Dhimitrios II: Ceramics, Objects, Tombs, Specialist Studies* (Studies in Mediterranean Archaeology 71:3). Göteborg: Paul Åströms.

Stanley Price, N. P. 1979. *Early Prehistoric Settlement in Cyprus: A Review and Gazetteer of Sites, c. 6500–3000 BC*. Oxford: British Archaeological Reports.

Symeonoglou, S. 1972. "Archaeological Survey in the Area of Phlamoudhi, Cyprus," *Report of the Department of Antiquities, Cyprus*: 187–98.

Symington, D. 1991. "Late Bronze Age Writing-boards and Their Uses: Textual Evidence from Anatolia and Syria," *Anatolian Studies* 41: 111–23.

Todd, I. A., and D. Pilides 2001. "The Archaeology of White Slip Production," 27–43, in V. Karageorghis ed., *The White Slip Ware of Late Bronze Age Cyprus*. Vienna: Österreichischen Akademie der Wissenschaften.

Vaughan, S. J. 1991a. "Late Cypriot Base Ring Ware: Studies in Raw Materials and Technology," 337–68, in A. Middleton and I. Freestone eds., *Recent Developments in Ceramic Petrology*. London: British Museum.

———1991b. "Material and Technical Classification of Base Ring Ware: A New Fabric Typology," 119–30, in J. A. Barlow, D. L. Bolger, and B. Kling eds., *Cypriot Ceramics: Reading the Prehistoric Record*. Philadelphia: University of Pennsylvania Press.

Vermeule, E. D. T., and F. Z. Wolsky 1990. *Toumba tou Skourou: A Bronze Age Potters' Quarter on Morphou Bay in Cyprus*. Cambridge: Harvard University Press.

Webb, J. M., and D. Frankel 1994. "Making an Impression: Storage and Surplus Finance in Late Bronze Age Cyprus," *Journal of Mediterranean Archaeology* 7: 5–26.

Weinberg, S. S. 1983. *Bamboula at Kourion: The Architecture*. Philadelphia: University of Pennsylvania Press.

Yon, M., V. Karageorghis, and N. Hirshfeld 2000. *Céramiques Mycéniennes d'Ougarit* (Ras Shamra-Ougarit 13). Nicosia: A. G. Leventis Foundation.